CSS
Pocket Reference

FOURTH EDITION

CSS
Pocket Reference

Eric A. Meyer

Beijing · Cambridge · Farnham · Köln · Sebastopol · Tokyo

CSS Pocket Reference, Fourth Edition

by Eric A. Meyer

Copyright © 2011 O'Reilly Media, Inc. All rights reserved.
Printed in Canada.

Published by O'Reilly Media, Inc., 1005 Gravenstein Highway North, Sebastopol, CA 95472.

O'Reilly books may be purchased for educational, business, or sales promotional use. Online editions are also available for most titles (*http://my.safari booksonline.com*). For more information, contact our corporate/institutional sales department: (800) 998-9938 or *corporate@oreilly.com*.

Editor: Simon St. Laurent
Production Editor: Teresa Elsey
Proofreader: Teresa Elsey
Indexer: Potomac Indexing, LLC
Cover Designer: Karen Montgomery
Interior Designer: David Futato
Illustrator: Robert Romano

Printing History:

May 2001:	First Edition.
July 2004:	Second Edition.
October 2007:	Third Edition.
July 2011:	Fourth Edition.

ISBN: 978-1-449-39903-0

[TM]

1310132081

Contents

Preface

Cascading Style Sheets (CSS) is the W3C standard for the visual presentation of web pages (although it can be used in other settings as well). After a short introduction to the key concepts of CSS, this pocket reference provides an alphabetical reference to all CSS3 selectors, followed by an alphabetical reference to CSS3 properties.

Conventions Used in This Book

The following typographical conventions are used in this book:

Italic

> Used to indicate new terms, URLs, filenames, file extensions, directories, commands and options, and program names. For example, a path in the filesystem will appear as *C:\windows\system*.

`Constant width`

> Used to show the contents of files or the output from commands.

`Constant width italic`

> Shows text that should be replaced with user-supplied values or by values determined by context.

Using Code Examples

This book is here to help you get your job done. In general, you may use the code in this book in your programs and documentation. You do not need to contact us for permission unless you're reproducing a significant portion of the code. For example, writing a program that uses several chunks of code from this book does not require permission. Selling or distributing a CD-ROM of examples from O'Reilly books does require permission. Answering a question by citing this book and quoting example code does not require permission. Incorporating a significant amount of example code from this book into your product's documentation does require permission.

We appreciate, but do not require, attribution. An attribution usually includes the title, author, publisher, and ISBN. For example: "*CSS Pocket Reference* by Eric A. Meyer (O'Reilly). Copyright 2011 O'Reilly Media, Inc., 978-1-449-39903-0."

If you feel your use of code examples falls outside fair use or the permission given above, feel free to contact us at *permissions@oreilly.com*.

Safari® Books Online

Safari Books Online is an on-demand digital library that lets you easily search over 7,500 technology and creative reference books and videos to find the answers you need quickly.

With a subscription, you can read any page and watch any video from our library online. Read books on your cell phone and mobile devices. Access new titles before they are available for print, and get exclusive access to manuscripts in development and post feedback for the authors. Copy and paste code samples, organize your favorites, download chapters, bookmark key sections, create notes, print out pages, and benefit from tons of other time-saving features.

O'Reilly Media has uploaded this book to the Safari Books Online service. To have full digital access to this book and others on similar topics from O'Reilly and other publishers, sign up for free at *http://my.safaribooksonline.com*.

How to Contact Us

Visit Eric A. Meyer's website at *http://meyerweb.com/* or follow @meyerweb on Twitter.

Please address comments and questions concerning this book to the publisher:

O'Reilly Media, Inc.
1005 Gravenstein Highway North
Sebastopol, CA 95472
800-998-9938 (in the United States or Canada)
707-829-0515 (international or local)
707-829-0104 (fax)

We have a web page for this book, where we list errata, examples, and any additional information. You can access this page at:

http://oreilly.com/catalog/9781449399030/

To comment or ask technical questions about this book, send email to:

bookquestions@oreilly.com

For more information about our books, courses, conferences, and news, see our website at *http://www.oreilly.com*.

Find us on Facebook: *http://facebook.com/oreilly*

Follow us on Twitter: *http://twitter.com/oreillymedia*

Watch us on YouTube: *http://www.youtube.com/oreillymedia*

CHAPTER 1

Basic Concepts

Adding Styles to HTML and XHTML

Styles can be applied to documents in three distinct ways, as discussed in the following sections.

Inline Styles

In HTML and XHTML, style information can be specified for an individual element via the `style` attribute. The value of a `style` attribute is a declaration block (see the section "Rule Structure" on page 5) without the curly braces:

```
<p style="color: red; background: yellow;">Look out!
This text is alarmingly presented!</p>
```

Note that, as of this writing, a full style sheet cannot be placed into a `style` attribute. Only the content of a single declaration block can be used as a `style` attribute value. For example, it is not possible to place hover styles (using `:hover`) in a `style` attribute, nor can one use `@import` in this context.

Although typical XML document languages (e.g., XHTML 1.0, XHTML 1.1, and SVG) support the `style` attribute, it is unlikely that all XML languages will support a similar capability. Because of this and because it encourages poor authoring practices, authors are generally discouraged from using the style attribute.

Embedded Style Sheets

A style sheet can be embedded at the top of an HTML or XHTML document using the **style** element, which must appear within the **head** element:

```
<html><head><title>Stylin'!</title>
<style type="text/css">
h1 {color: purple;}
p {font-size: smaller; color: gray;}
</style>
</head>
    ...
</html>
```

XML languages may or may not provide an equivalent capability; always check the language DTD to be certain.

External Style Sheets

Styles can be listed in a separate file. The primary advantage to a separate file is that by collecting commonly used styles in a single file, all pages using that style sheet can be updated by editing a single style sheet. Another key advantage is that external style sheets are cached, which can help reduce bandwidth usage. An external style sheet can be referenced in one of the following three ways:

@import directive

One or more **@import** directives can be placed at the beginning of any style sheet. For HTML and XHTML documents, this would be done within an embedded style sheet:

```
<head><title>My Document</title>
<style type="text/css">
@import url(site.css);
@import url(navbar.css);
@import url(footer.css);
body {background: yellow;}
```

```
</style>
</head>
```

Note that @import directives can appear at the top (and, according to the specification, *only* at the top) of any style sheet. Thus, one style sheet could import another, which in turn would import a third.

link element

In HTML and XHTML documents, the link element can be used to associate a style sheet with a document. Multiple link elements are permitted. The media attribute can be used to restrict a style sheet to one or more media:

```
<head>
<title>A Document</title>
<link rel="stylesheet" type="text/css" href="basic.css"
  media="all">
<link rel="stylesheet" type="text/css" href="web.css"
  media="screen">
<link rel="stylesheet" type="text/css" href="paper.css"
  media="print">
</head>
```

It is also possible to link to alternate style sheets. If alternate style sheets are supplied, it is up to the user agent (or the author) to provide a means for the user to select one of the alternates:

```
<head>
<title>A Document</title>
<link rel="stylesheet" type="text/css" href="basic.css">
<link rel="alternate stylesheet" title="Classic"
  type="text/css" href="oldschool.css">
<link rel="alternate stylesheet" title="Futuristic"
  type="text/css" href="3000ad.css">
</head>
```

As of this writing, most or all known user agents load all linked style sheets, including the alternate style sheets, regardless of whether the user ever implements them. This can have implications for bandwidth use and server load.

xml-stylesheet processing instruction

In XML documents (such as XHTML documents sent with a mime-type of "text/xml," "application/xml," or "application/xhtml+xml"), an xml-stylesheet processing instruction can be used to associate a style sheet with a document. Any xml-stylesheet processing instructions must be placed in the prolog of an XML document. Multiple xml-stylesheet processing instructions are permitted. The media pseudo-attribute can be used to restrict a style sheet to one or more forms of media:

```
<?xml-stylesheet type="text/css" href="basic.css"
  media="all"?>
<?xml-stylesheet type="text/css" href="web.css"
  media="screen"?>
<?xml-stylesheet type="text/css" href="paper.css"
  media="print"?>
```

It is also possible to link to alternate style sheets with the xml-stylesheet processing instruction:

```
<?xml-stylesheet type="text/css" href="basic.css"?>
<?xml-stylesheet alternate="yes" title="Classic"
  type="text/css" href="oldschool.css"?>
<?xml-stylesheet alternate="yes" title="Futuristic"
  type="text/css" href="3000ad.css"?>
```

HTTP Link headers

The last (and least common by far) way of associating an external style sheet with your pages is to use an HTTP Link header. In CSS terms, this is a way of replicating the effects of a link element using HTTP headers.

Adding a line such as this to the .htaccess file at the root level of your server will make this happen for all pages on the site:

```
Header add Link
  "</style.css>;rel=stylesheet;type=text/css;media=all"
```

As an alternative to using .htaccess, which has been known to cause performance hits, you can edit your httpd.conf file to do the same thing:

```
<Directory /usr/local/username/httpdocs>
Header add Link
```

```
    "</ style.css>;rel=stylesheet;type=text/css;media=all"
  </Directory>
```

...where **/usr/local/username/httpdocs** is replaced with the
UNIX pathname of your website's actual home directory.

As of this writing, HTTP headers were not supported by all
user agents, most notably Internet Explorer and Safari. Thus,
this technique is usually limited to production environments
based on other user agents and the occasional Easter egg for
Firefox and Opera users.

Rule Structure

A style sheet consists of one or more rules that describe
how page elements should be presented. Every *rule* has two
fundamental parts: the *selector* and the *declaration block*.
Figure 1-1 illustrates the structure of a rule.

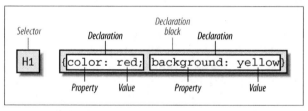

Figure 1-1. Rule structure

On the left side of the rule, we find the selector, which selects
the parts of the document to which the rule should be applied.
On the right side of the rule, we have the declaration block.
A declaration block is made up of one or more *declarations*;
each declaration is a combination of a CSS *property* and a
value of that property.

The declaration block is always enclosed in curly braces. A
declaration block can contain several declarations; each declaration must be terminated with a semicolon (;). The exception is the final declaration in a declaration block, for which
the semicolon is optional.

Each property, which represents a particular stylistic parameter, is separated from its value by a colon (:). Property names in CSS are not case-sensitive. Legal values for a property are defined by the property description. Chapter 4 provides details on acceptable values for CSS properties.

Comments

Including comments in CSS is simple. You open with /* and end with */, like this:

```
/* This is a comment! */
```

Comments can be multiple lines long:

```
/* This is a comment!
  This is a continuation of the comment.
 And so is this. */
```

They can also occur anywhere within a style sheet except in the middle of a token (property name or value):

```
h1/* heading-level-1 */ {color /* foreground color */:
    rgba(23,58,89,0.42) /* RGB + opacity */;}
```

HTML (properly SGML) comments (<!-- such as this -->) are permitted in style sheets so as to hide the styles from browsers so old that they don't understand HTML 3.2. They do *not* act as CSS comments; that is, anything contained in an HTML comment will be seen and interpreted by the CSS parser.

Style Precedence

A single HTML or XHTML document can import and link to multiple external style sheets, contain one or more embedded style sheets, and make use of inline styles. In the process, it is quite possible that some rules will conflict with one another. CSS uses a mechanism called the *cascade* to resolve any such conflicts and arrive at a final set of styles to be applied to the document. Two key components of the cascade are *specificity* and *inheritance*.

Specificity Calculations

Specificity describes the weight of a selector and any declarations associated with it. The following table summarizes the components of specificity summation.

Selector type	Example	Specificity
Universal selector	*	0,0,0,0
Combinator	+	
Element identifier	div	0,0,0,1
Pseudo-element identifier	::first-line	
Class identifier	.warning	0,0,1,0
Pseudo-class identifier	:hover	
Attribute identifier	[type="checkbox"]	
ID identifier	#content	0,1,0,0
Inline style attribute	style="color: red;"	1,0,0,0

Specificity values are cumulative; thus, a selector containing two element identifiers and a class identifier (e.g., `div.aside p`) has a specificity of 0,0,1,2. Specificity values are sorted in right-to-left precedence; thus, a selector containing 11 element identifiers (0,0,0,11) has a lower specificity than a selector containing just a single class identifier (0,0,1,0).

The `!important` directive gives a declaration more weight than nonimportant declarations. The declaration retains the specificity of its selectors and is used only in comparison with other important declarations.

Inheritance

The elements in a document form a treelike hierarchy with the root element at the top and the rest of the document structure spreading out below it (which makes it look more like a tree root system, really). In an HTML document, the html element is at the top of the tree, with the head and body elements descending from it. The rest of the document structure descends from those elements. In such a structure, elements lower down in the tree are descendants of the ancestors, which are higher in the tree.

CSS uses the document tree for the mechanism of *inheritance*, in which a style applied to an element is inherited by its descendants. For example, if the body element is set to have a color of red, that value propagates down the document tree to the elements that descend from the body element. Inheritance is interrupted only by a style rule that applies directly to an element. Inherited values have no specificity at all (which is *not* the same as having zero specificity).

Note that some elements are not inherited. A property will always define whether it is inherited. Some examples of noninherited properties are padding, border, margin, and background.

The Cascade

The cascade is how CSS resolves conflicts between styles; in other words, it is the mechanism by which a user agent decides, for example, what color to make an element when two different rules apply to it and each one tries to set a different color. The following steps constitute the cascade:

1. Find all declarations that contain a selector that matches a given element.

2. Sort by explicit weight all declarations applying to the element. Those rules marked !important are given greater weight than those that are not. Also, sort by origin all declarations applying to a given element. There are three origins: author, reader, and user agent. Under normal circumstances, the author's styles win out over the reader's styles. !important reader styles are stronger than any other

styles, including `!important` author styles. Both author and reader styles override the user agent's default styles.

3. Sort by specificity all declarations applying to a given element. Those elements with a higher specificity have more weight than those with lower specificity.

4. Sort by order all declarations applying to a given element. The later a declaration appears in a style sheet or a document, the more weight it is given. Declarations that appear in an imported style sheet are considered to come before all declarations within the style sheet that imports them, and have a lower weight than those in the importing style sheet.

Any presentational hints that come from non-CSS sources (e.g., the preference dialog within a browser) are given the same weight as the user agent's default styles (see step 2 above).

Element Classification

Broadly speaking, CSS groups elements into two types: *nonreplaced* and *replaced*. Although the types may seem rather abstract, there actually are some profound differences in how the two types of elements are presented. These differences are explored in detail in Chapter 7 of *CSS: The Definitive Guide*, third edition (O'Reilly).

Nonreplaced Elements

The majority of HTML and XHTML elements are *nonreplaced elements*, which means their content is presented by the user agent inside a box generated by the element itself. For example, `<span>hi there</span>` is a nonreplaced element, and the text `hi there` will be displayed by the user agent. Paragraphs, headings, table cells, lists, and almost everything else in HTML and XHTML are nonreplaced elements.

Replaced Elements

In contrast, *replaced elements* are those whose content is replaced by something not directly represented by document content. The most familiar HTML example is the `img` element, which is replaced by an image file external to the document itself. In fact, `img` itself has no actual content, as we can see by considering a simple example:

```
<img src="howdy.gif" alt="Hi">
```

There is no content contained in the element—only an element name and attributes. Only by replacing the element's lack of content with content found through other means (in this case, loading an external image specified by the `src` attribute) can the element have any presentation at all. Another example is the `input` element, which may be replaced with a radio button, checkbox, or text input box, depending on its type. Replaced elements also generate boxes in their display.

Element Display Roles

In addition to being replaced or not, there are two basic types of element display roles in CSS3: *block-level* and *inline-level*. All CSS3 `display` values fall into one of these two categories. It can be important to know which general role a box falls into, since some properties only apply to one type or the other.

Block-Level

Block-level boxes are those where the element box (by default) fills its parent element's content area width and cannot have other elements to its sides. In other words, block-level elements generate "breaks" before and after the element box. The most familiar block elements from HTML are `p` and `div`. Replaced elements can be block-level elements but usually are not.

List items are a special case of block-level elements. In addition to behaving in a manner consistent with other block elements, they generate a marker—typically a bullet for unordered lists or a number for ordered lists—which is "attached" to the element box. Except for the presence of this marker, list items are identical to other block elements.

The `display` values that create block boxes are: `block`, `list-item`, `table`, `table-row-group`, `table-header-group`, `table-footer-group`, `table-row`, `table-column-group`, `table-column`, `table-cell`, `table-caption`, and (as of this writing) all CSS Advanced Layout templates.

Inline-Level

Inline-level boxes are those where an element box is generated within a line of text and does not break up the flow of that line. Perhaps the best-known inline element is the `a` element in HTML and XHTML. Other examples are `span` and `em`. These elements do not generate a break before or after themselves, so they can appear within the content of another element without disrupting its display.

Note that although the CSS block and inline elements have a great deal in common with HTML and XHTML block- and inline-level elements, there is an important difference. In HTML and XHTML, block-level elements cannot descend from inline-level elements, whereas in CSS, there is no restriction on how display roles can be nested within each other.

The `display` values that create inline boxes are: `inline`, `inline-block`, `inline-table`, and `ruby`. As of this writing, it was not explicitly defined that the various Ruby-related values (e.g., `ruby-text`) also generate inline boxes, but this seems the most likely outcome.

Run-In

A special case is *run-in boxes*, defined by `display: run-in`, which can generate either a block or an inline box depending on the situation. The rules that decide the outcome are:

1. If the run-in itself contains a block box, the run-in generates a block box.
2. If that's not the case, and the run-in is immediately followed by a sibling block box that is neither floated nor absolutely positioned, the run-in box becomes the first inline box of the sibling block box.
3. If neither condition applies, the run-in generates a block box.

In the case where a run-in is inserted as the first inline of its sibling block box (rule 2 above), it does *not* inherit property values from that block box. Instead, it continues to inherit from its structural parent element. Thus, if the sibling block box has `color: green` applied to it, the green will not be inherited by the run-in element even though it is visually a part of the block box.

Basic Visual Layout

CSS defines algorithms for laying out any element in a document. These algorithms form the underpinnings of visual presentation in CSS. There are two primary kinds of layout, each with very different behaviors: block-level and inline-level layout.

Block-Level Layout

A block-level box in CSS generates a rectangular box called the *element box*, which describes the amount of space occupied by an element. Figure 1-2 shows the various components of an element box. The following rules apply to an element box:

- The background of the element box extends to the outer edge of the border, thus filling the content, padding, and border areas. If the border has any transparent portions (e.g., it is dotted or dashed), the background will be visible in those portions. The background does not extend into the margin areas of the box. Any outlines are drawn in the margin area and do not affect layout.

- Only the margins, `height`, and `width` of an element box may be set to `auto`.
- Only margins can be given negative values.
- The padding and border widths of the element box default to `0` (zero) and `none`, respectively.
- If `box-sizing` is `content-box` (the default value), the property `width` defines only the width of the content area; any padding, borders, or margins are added to it. The same is true for `height` with respect to the height.
- If `box-sizing` is `border-box`, the property `width` defines the total width of the content, padding, and borders; any margins are added to it. The same is true for `height` with respect to the height.

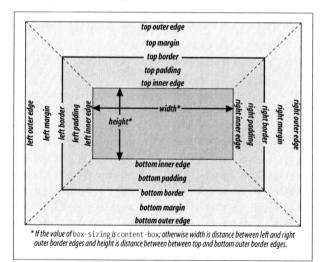

* If the value of box-sizing is content-box; otherwise width is distance between left and right outer border edges and height is distance between between top and bottom outer border edges.

Figure 1-2. Box model details

Inline Layout

An inline-level box in CSS generates one or more rectangular boxes called *inline boxes*, depending on whether the inline box is broken across multiple lines. The following rules apply to inline box:

- For the properties `left`, `right`, `top`, `bottom`, `margin-left`, `margin-right`, `margin-top`, and `margin-bottom`, any value of `auto` is converted to 0 (zero).

- `width` and `height` do not apply to nonreplaced inline boxes.

- For replaced inline boxes, the following rules apply:

  — If `height` and `width` are both `auto` and the element has an intrinsic width (e.g., an image), that value of `width` is equal to the element's intrinsic width. The same holds true for `height`.

  — If `height` and `width` are both `auto` and the element does not have an intrinsic width but does have an intrinsic height and layout ratio, then `width` is set to be the intrinsic height times the ratio.

  — If `height` and `width` are both `auto` and the element does not have an intrinsic height but does have an intrinsic width and layout ratio, then `height` is set to be the intrinsic width divided by the ratio.

There are a few rules even more obscure than those last two, which are too lengthy to include here; see *http://w3.org/TR/css3 -box/#inline-replaced* for details.

All inline elements have a `line-height`, which has a great deal to do with how the elements are displayed. The height of a line of text is determined by taking into account the following factors:

Anonymous text
　　Any string of characters not contained within an inline element. Thus, in the markup:

```
<p> I'm <em>so</em> happy!</p>
```

...the sequences "I'm " and " happy!" are anonymous text. Note that the spaces are part of the anonymous text, as a space is a character like any other.

Em-box

The em-box defined in the given font; otherwise known as the character box. Actual glyphs can be taller or shorter than their em-boxes, as discussed in Chapter 5 of *CSS: The Definitive Guide*, third edition (O'Reilly). In CSS, the value of `font-size` determines the height of each em-box.

Content area

In nonreplaced elements, the content area can be the box described by the em-boxes of every character in the element, strung together, or else the box described by the character glyphs in the element. The CSS2.1 specification allows user agents to choose either. This text uses the em-box definition for simplicity's sake. In replaced elements, the content area is the intrinsic height of the element plus any margins, borders, or padding.

Leading

The leading is the difference between the values of `font-size` and `line-height`. Half this difference is applied to the top and half to the bottom of the content area. These additions to the content area are called, not surprisingly, half-leading. Leading is applied only to nonreplaced elements.

Inline box

The box described by the addition of the leading to the content area. For nonreplaced elements, the height of the inline box of an element will be equal to the value for `line-height`. For replaced elements, the height of the inline box of an element will be equal to the content area, as leading is not applied to replaced elements.

Line box

The shortest box that bounds the highest and lowest points of the inline boxes that are found in the line. In other words, the top edge of the line box will be placed along the top of the highest inline box top, and the bottom of the line box is placed along the bottom of the lowest inline box bottom. (See Figure 1-3.)

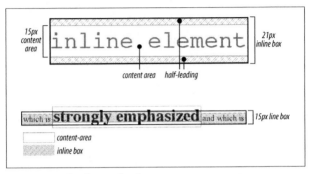

Figure 1-3. Inline layout details

Floating

Floating allows an element to be placed to the left or right of its containing block (which is the nearest block-level ancestor element), with following content flowing around the element. Any floated element automatically generates a block box, regardless of what type of box it would generate if not floated. A floated element is placed according to the following rules:

- The left (or right) outer edge of a floated element may not be to the left (or right) of the inner edge of its containing block.

- The left (or right) outer edge of a floated element must be to the right (or left) of the right (left) outer edge of a left-floating (or right-floating) element that occurs earlier in the document's source, unless the top of the later element is below the bottom of the former.

- The right outer edge of a left-floating element may not be to the right of the left outer edge of any right-floating element to its right. The left outer edge of a right-floating element may not be to the left of the right outer edge of any left-floating element to its left.

- A floating element's top may not be higher than the inner top of its containing block.

- A floating element's top may not be higher than the top of any earlier floating or block-level element.

- A floating element's top may not be higher than the top of any line box with content that precedes the floating element.

- A left (or right) floating element that has another floating element to its left (right) may not have its right (left) outer edge to the right (left) of its containing block's right (left) edge.

- A floating element must be placed as high as possible.

- A left-floating element must be put as far to the left as possible, and a right-floating element as far to the right as possible. A higher position is preferred to one that is farther to the right or left.

Positioning

When elements are positioned, a number of special rules come into play. These rules govern not only the containing block of the element, but also how it is laid out within that element.

Types of Positioning

Static positioning
> The element's box is generated as normal. Block-level elements generate a rectangular box that is part of the document's flow, and inline-level boxes generate one or more line boxes that flow within their parent element.

Relative positioning

> The element's box is offset by some distance. Its containing block can be considered to be the area that the element would occupy if it were not positioned. The element retains the shape it would have had were it not positioned, and the space that the element would ordinarily have occupied is preserved.

Absolute positioning

> The element's box is completely removed from the flow of the document and positioned with respect to its containing block, which may be another element in the document or the initial containing block (described in the next section). Whatever space the element might have occupied in the normal document flow is closed up, as though the element did not exist. The positioned element generates a block box, regardless of the type of box it would generate if it were in the normal flow.

Fixed positioning

> The element's box behaves as though set to `absolute`, but its containing block is the viewport itself.

The Containing Block

The containing block of a positioned element is determined as follows:

1. The containing block of the *root element* (also called the *initial containing block*) is established by the user agent. In HTML, the root element is the `html` element, although some browsers may use `body`.

2. For nonroot elements, if an element's `position` value is `relative` or `static`, its containing block is formed by the content edge of the nearest block-level, table-, cell-, or inline-block ancestor box. Despite this rule, relatively positioned elements are still simply offset, not positioned with respect to the containing block described here, and statically positioned elements do not move from their place in the normal flow.

3. For nonroot elements that have a **position** value of **absolute**, the containing block is set to the nearest ancestor (of any kind) that has a **position** value other than **static**. This happens as follows:

   a. If the ancestor is block-level, the containing block is that element's outer padding edge; in other words, it is the area bounded by the element's border.

   b. If the ancestor is inline-level, the containing block is set to the content edge of the ancestor. In left-to-right languages, the top and left of the containing block are the top and left content edges of the first box in the ancestor, and the bottom and right edges are the bottom and right content edges of the last box. In right-to-left languages, the right edge of the containing block corresponds to the right content edge of the first box, and the left is taken from the last box. The top and bottom are the same.

   c. If there are no ancestors as described in 3a and 3b, the absolutely positioned element's containing block is defined to be the initial containing block.

Layout of Absolutely Positioned Elements

In the following sections, these terms are used:

Shrink-to-fit
> Similar to calculating the width of a table cell using the automatic table layout algorithm. In general, the user agent attempts to find the minimum element width that will contain the content and wrap to multiple lines only if wrapping cannot be avoided.

Static position
> The place where an element's edge would have been placed if its **position** were **static**.

Horizontal layout of absolutely positioned elements

The equation that governs the layout of these elements is:

```
left + margin-left + border-left-width + padding-left +
width + padding-right + border-right-width +
margin-right + right + vertical scrollbar width (if any) =
width of containing block
```

The width of any vertical scrollbar is determined by the user agent and cannot be affected with CSS.

For *nonreplaced* elements, the steps used to determine horizontal layout are:

1. If all of `left`, `width`, and `right` are `auto`, first reset any `auto` values for `margin-left` and `margin-right` to 0. Then, if `direction` is `ltr`, set `left` to the static position and apply the rule given in step 3c. Otherwise, set `right` to the static position and apply the rule given in step 3a.

2. If none of `left`, `width`, and `right` is `auto`, pick the rule that applies from the following list:

   a. If both `margin-left` and `margin-right` are set to `auto`, solve the equation under the additional constraint that the two margins get equal values.

   b. If only one of `margin-left` or `margin-right` is set to `auto`, solve the equation for that value.

   c. If the values are overconstrained (none is set to `auto`), ignore the value for `left` if `direction` is `rtl` (ignore `right` if `direction` is `ltr`) and solve for that value.

3. If some of `left`, `width`, and `right` are `auto`, but others are not, reset any `auto` values for `margin-left` and `margin-right` to 0. From the following list, pick the one rule that applies:

   a. If `left` and `width` are `auto` and `right` is not, the width is shrink-to-fit. Solve the equation for `left`.

   b. If `left` and `right` are `auto` and `width` is not, then if `direction` is `ltr`, set `left` to the static position (otherwise, set `right` to the static position). Solve the equation for `left` (if direction is `rtl`) or `right` (if `direction` is `ltr`).

c. If `width` and `right` are `auto` and `left` is not, the width is shrink-to-fit. Solve the equation for `right`.

d. If `left` is `auto` and `width` and `right` are not, solve the equation for `left`.

e. If `width` is `auto` and `left` and `right` are not, solve the equation for `width`.

f. If `right` is `auto` and `left` and `width` are not, solve the equation for `right`.

For *replaced* elements, the steps used to determine horizontal layout are:

1. Determine the value of `width` as described for inline replaced elements (see "Inline Layout" on page 14).

2. If both `left` and `right` are set to `auto`, then if `direction` is `ltr`, set `left` to the static left position. If `direction` is `rtl`, set `right` to the static right position.

3. If either or both of `left` and `right` are set to `auto`, reset any `auto` values for `margin-left` and `margin-right` to 0.

4. If neither `left` nor `right` is set to `auto` and both `margin-left` and `margin-right` are set to `auto`, solve the equation under the additional constraint that the two margins get equal values.

5. If the values are overconstrained (none is set to `auto`), ignore the value for `left` if `direction` is `rtl` (ignore `right` if `direction` is `ltr`) and solve for that value.

Vertical layout of absolutely positioned elements

The equation that governs the layout of these elements is:

```
top + margin-top + border-top-width + padding-top + height
+ padding-bottom + border-bottom-width + margin-bottom +
bottom + horizontal scrollbar height (if any) =
height of containing block
```

The height of any horizontal scrollbar is determined by the user agent and cannot be affected with CSS.

For *nonreplaced* elements, the steps used to determine vertical layout are:

1. If all of `top`, `height`, and `bottom` are `auto`, set `top` to the static position and apply the rule given in step 3c.

2. If none of `top`, `height`, and `bottom` is `auto`, pick the one rule that applies from the following list:

   a. If both `margin-top` and `margin-bottom` are set to `auto`, solve the equation under the additional constraint that the two margins get equal values.

   b. If only one of `margin-top` or `margin-bottom` is set to `auto`, solve the equation for that value.

   c. If the values are overconstrained (none is set to `auto`), ignore the value for `bottom` and solve for that value.

3. If some of `top`, `height`, and `bottom` are `auto`, but others are not, pick the one rule that applies from the following list:

   a. If `top` and `height` are `auto` and `bottom` is not, the height is based on the element's content (as it would be in the static flow). Reset any `auto` values for `margin-top` and `margin-bottom` to 0 and solve the equation for `top`.

   b. If `top` and `bottom` are `auto` and `height` is not, set `top` to the static position. Reset any `auto` values for `margin-top` and `margin-bottom` to 0 and solve the equation for `bottom`.

   c. If `height` and `bottom` are `auto` and `top` is not, the height is based on the element's content (as it would be in the static flow). Reset any `auto` values for `margin-top` and `margin-bottom` to 0 and solve the equation for `bottom`.

   d. If `top` is `auto` and `height` and `bottom` are not, reset any `auto` values for `margin-top` and `margin-bottom` to 0 and solve the equation for `top`.

   e. If `height` is `auto` and `top` and `bottom` are not, reset any `auto` values for `margin-top` and `margin-bottom` to 0 and solve the equation for `height`.

f. If `bottom` is `auto` and `top` and `height` are not, reset any `auto` values for `margin-top` and `margin-bottom` to 0 and solve the equation for `bottom`.

For *replaced* elements, the steps used to determine vertical layout are:

1. Determine the value of `height` as described for inline replaced elements (see "Inline Layout" on page 14).

2. If both `top` and `bottom` are set to `auto`, set `top` to the static top position.

3. If the values are overconstrained, ignore the value for `bottom` and solve for that value.

Table Layout

The layout of tables can get quite complicated, especially because CSS defines two different ways to calculate table and cell widths, as well as two ways to handle the borders of tables and elements internal to the table. Figure 1-4 illustrates the components of a table.

Table Arrangement Rules

In general, a table is laid out according to the following principles:

- Each row box encompasses a single row of grid cells. All of the row boxes in a table fill the table from top to bottom in the order they occur in the source document. Thus, the table contains as many grid rows as there are row elements.

- A row group's box encompasses the same grid cells as the row boxes that it contains.

- A column box encompasses one or more columns of grid cells. Column boxes are placed next to each other in the order they occur. The first column box is on the left for left-to-right languages and on the right for right-to-left languages.

- A column group's box encompasses the same grid cells as the column boxes that it contains.

- Although cells may span several rows or columns, CSS does not define how that happens. It is instead left to the document language to define spanning. Each spanned cell is a rectangular box one or more grid cells wide and high. The top row of this rectangle is in the row that is parent to the cell. The cell's rectangle must be as far to the left as possible in left-to-right languages, but it may not overlap any other cell box. It must also be to the right of all cells in the same row that are earlier in the source document in a left-to-right language. In right-to-left languages, a spanned cell must be as far to the right as possible without overlapping other cells and must be to the left of all cells in the same row that come after it in the document source.

- A cell's box cannot extend beyond the last row box of a table or row group. If the table structure causes this condition, the cell must be shortened until it fits within the table or row group that encloses it.

Fixed Table Layout

The fixed-layout model is fast because its layout doesn't depend on the contents of table cells; it's driven by the `width` values of the table, columns, and cells within the first row of the table. The fixed-layout model uses the following simple steps:

1. Any column element whose `width` property has a value other than `auto` sets the width for that column.

2. If a column has an `auto` width, but the cell in the first row of the table within that column has a `width` other than `auto`, that cell sets the width for that column. If the cell

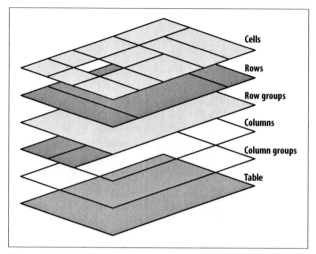

Figure 1-4. Table layout components

spans multiple columns, the width is divided equally among the columns.

3. Any columns that are still auto-sized are sized so that their widths are as equal as possible.

At that point, the width of the table is set to be either the value of `width` for the table or the sum of the column widths, whichever is greater. If the table turns out to be wider than the column widths, the difference is divided by the number of columns and added to each of them.

Automatic Table Layout

The automatic-layout model, although not as fast as the fixed-layout, is likely to be much more familiar to authors because it's substantially the same model that HTML tables have used for years. In most current user agents, use of this model will be triggered by a table with a `width` of `auto`, regardless of the value of `table-layout`—although this is not assured.

The details of the model can be expressed in the following steps:

1. For each cell in a column, calculate both the minimum and maximum cell width.

2. Determine the minimum width required to display the content. In determining the minimum content width, the content can flow to any number of lines, but it may not stick out of the cell's box. If the cell has a `width` value that is larger than the minimum possible width, the minimum cell width is set to the value of `width`. If the cell's `width` value is `auto`, the minimum cell width is set to the minimum content width.

3. For the maximum width, determine the width required to display the content without any line-breaking, other than that forced by explicit line-breaking (e.g., due to the `<br>` element). That value is the maximum cell width.

4. For each column, calculate both the minimum and maximum column width.

   a. The column's minimum width is determined by the largest minimum cell width of the cells within the column. If the column has been given an explicit `width` value that is larger than any of the minimum cell widths within the column, the minimum column width is set to the value of `width`.

   b. For the maximum width, take the largest maximum cell width of the cells within the column. If the column has been given an explicit `width` value that is larger than any of the maximum cell widths within the column, the maximum column width is set to the value of `width`. These two behaviors recreate the traditional HTML table behavior of forcibly expanding any column to be as wide as its widest cell.

5. In cases where a cell spans more than one column, the sum of the minimum column widths must be equal to the minimum cell width for the spanning cell. Similarly, the sum of the maximum column widths must equal the spanning

cell's maximum width. User agents should divide any changes in column widths equally among the spanned columns.

In addition, the user agent must take into account that when a column width has a percentage value for its `width`, the percentage is calculated in relation to the width of the table—even though that width is not known yet. The user agent must hang on to the percentage value and use it in the next part of the algorithm. Once the user agent has determined how wide or narrow each column can be, it can calculate the width of the table. This happens as follows:

1. If the computed width of the table is not `auto`, the computed table width is compared to the sum of all the column widths plus any borders and cell-spacing. (Columns with percentage widths are likely calculated at this time.) The larger of the two values is the final width of the table. If the table's computed width is larger than the sum of the column widths, borders, and cell-spacing, all columns are increased in width by an equal amount so they fill the computed width of the table.

2. If the computed width of the table is `auto`, the final width of the table is determined by summing up the column widths, borders, and cell-spacing. This means the table will be only as wide as needed to display its content, just as with traditional HTML tables. Any columns with percentage widths use that percentage as a constraint, but it is a constraint that a user agent does not have to satisfy.

Once the last step is completed, then (and only then) can the user agent actually lay out the table.

Collapsing Cell Borders

The collapsing cell model largely describes how HTML tables have always been laid out when they have no cell-spacing. The following rules govern this model:

- Table elements cannot have any padding, although they can have margins. Thus, there is never separation between the border around the outside of the table and its outermost cells.

- Borders can be applied to cells, rows, row groups, columns, and column groups. The `table` element itself can, as always, have a border.

- There is never any separation between cell borders. In fact, borders collapse into each other where they adjoin so that only one of the collapsing borders is actually drawn. This is somewhat akin to margin-collapsing, where the largest margin wins. When cell borders collapse, the "most interesting" border wins.

- Once they are collapsed, the borders between cells are centered on the hypothetical grid lines between the cells.

Collapsing borders

When two or more borders are adjacent, they collapse into each other, as shown in Figure 1-5. There are strict rules governing which borders will win and which will not:

1. If one of the collapsing borders has a `border-style` of `hidden`, it takes precedence over all other collapsing borders: all borders at this location are hidden.

2. If one of the collapsing borders has a `border-style` of `none`, it takes the lowest priority. There will be no border drawn at this location only if all of the borders meeting at this location have a value of `none`. Note that `none` is the default value for `border-style`.

3. If at least one of the collapsing borders has a value other than either `none` or `hidden`, narrow borders lose out to wider ones. If two or more of the collapsing borders have the same width, the border style is taken in the following order, from most preferred to least: `double`, `solid`, `dashed`, `dotted`, `ridge`, `outset`, `groove`, `inset`. Thus, if two borders with the same width collapse and one is `dashed` while the other is `outset`, the border at that location will be dashed.

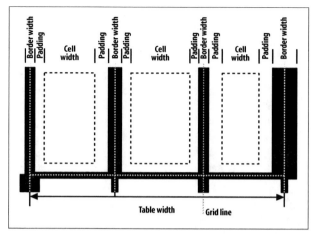

Figure 1-5. Collapsing cell borders model

4. If collapsing borders have the same style and width but differ in color, the color used is taken from an element in the following list, from most preferred to least: cell, row, row group, column, column group, table. Thus, if the borders of a cell and a column—identical in every way except color—collapse, the cell's border color (and style and width) will be used. If the collapsing borders come from the same type of element—such as two row borders with the same style and width, but different colors—the one farthest to the left and top wins in left-to-right languages; in right-to-left languages, the cell farthest to the right and top wins.

Vertical Alignment Within Cells

The following describes the detailed process for aligning cell contents within a row:

1. If any of the cells are baseline-aligned, the row's baseline is determined and the content of the baseline-aligned cells is placed.

2. Any top-aligned cell has its content placed. The row now has a provisional height, which is defined by the lowest cell bottom of the cells that have already had their content placed.

3. If any remaining cells are middle- or bottom-aligned, and the content height is taller than the provisional row height, the height of the row is increased by lowering the baseline in order to enclose the tallest of those cells.

4. All remaining cells have their content placed. In any cell with contents shorter than the row height, the cell's padding is increased in order to match the height of the row.

CHAPTER 2

Values

There are a variety of value types in CSS, most of which use units. Combining basic value types (such as numbers) with units (such as pixels) makes it possible to do any number of interesting things with CSS.

Keywords

Keywords are defined on a per-property basis and have a meaning specific only to a given property. For example, `normal` has totally unique meanings for the properties `font-variant` and `letter-spacing`. Keywords, like property names, are not case-sensitive. A special case is the keyword `inherit`, which is allowed on all properties and always has the same meaning (get the associated property's value from the element's parent). There is a second special universal keyword, `initial`, which is meant to represent the initial or default value for a given property. Thus, declaring `font-family: initial` would return the browser's preferences-based default font family. (Times, for most people.) The status and application of `initial` is unclear as of this writing and may be unreliable.

Color Values

#RRGGBB

>   This is a hex-pair notation familiar to authors using tra-
>   ditional HTML. In this format, the first pair of digits cor-
>   responds to the red level, the second pair to the green, and
>   the third pair to the blue. Each pair is in hexadecimal
>   notation in the range 00-FF. Thus, a "pure" blue is written
>   #0000FF, a "pure" red is written #FF0000, and so on.

#RGB

>   This is a shorter form of the six-digit notation described
>   previously. In this format, each digit is replicated to arrive
>   at an equivalent six-digit value; thus, #F8C becomes
>   #FF88CC.

rgb(rrr,ggg,bbb)

>   This format allows the author to use RGB values in the
>   range 0-255; only integers are permitted. Not coinciden-
>   tally, this range is the decimal equivalent of 00-FF in
>   hexadecimal. In this format, "pure" green is rgb
>   (0,255,0), and white is represented as rgb (255,255,255).

rgb(rrr.rr%,ggg.gg%,bbb.bb%)

>   This format allows the author to use RGB values in the
>   range 0% to 100%, with decimal values allowed (e.g.,
>   75.5%). The value for black is thus rgb (0%,0%,0%),
>   whereas "pure" blue is rgb (0%,0%,100%).

hsl(hhh.hh,sss.ss%,lll.ll%)

>   This format permits authors to specify a color by its hue
>   angle, saturation, and lightness (thus HSL). The hue angle
>   is always a unitless number in the range 0 to 360 and the
>   saturation and brightness values are always percentages.
>   Hue angles 0 and 360 are equivalent, and are both red. Hue
>   angles greater than 360 can be declared but they are nor-
>   malized to the 0–360 range; thus, setting a hue angle of
>   454 is equivalent to setting an angle of 94. Any HSL value,
>   regardless of color angle, will be rendered as a shade of
>   gray if the saturation value is 0%; the exact shade will de-
>   pend on the lightness value. Any HSL value, regardless of

the hue angle, will be rendered solid black if lightness is 0% and solid white if lightness is 100%. The "normal" lightness value—that is, the value associated with most common colors—is 50%.

rgba(rrr,ggg,bbb,a.aa)
rgba(rrr.rr%,ggg.gg%,bbb.bb%,a.aa)
hsla(hhh.hh,sss.ss%,lll.ll%,a.aa)

This extends the previous three formats to include an alpha (opacity) value. The alpha value must be a real number between 0 and 1 inclusive; percentages are not permitted for the alpha value. Thus, `rgba(0,0,255,0.5)` and `rgba(0,0,100%,0.5)` and `hsla(0,100%,50%,0.5)` are equivalent half-opaque red. There is no hexadecimal notation for RGBA.

<keyword>

One of 17 recognized keywords based largely on the original Windows VGA colors. These keywords are `aqua`, `black`, `blue`, `fuchsia`, `gray`, `green`, `lime`, `maroon`, `navy`, `olive`, `orange`, `purple`, `red`, `silver`, `teal`, `white`, and `yellow`. Browsers generally also recognize other keywords, such as the 147 X11 color keywords documented in section 4.3 of the W3C CSS3 Color Module specification (*http://www.w3.org/TR/css3-color*). The CSS3 Color Module drops `orange` from the list of recognized basic keywords, but it appears in the X11 list and all known browsers support it for historical reasons.

currentColor

A special keyword that represents the current computed value of the element's `color` property. This means that you could declare `background-color: currentColor` and set the element's background the same color as its foreground (not recommended). When applied to the `color` property, it is equivalent to declaring `color: inherit`. It can also be used on borders; `border: 1px solid` is equivalent to `border: 1px solid currentColor`. This can be quite useful when (un)setting a border's color via DOM scripting.

transparent

> A special keyword that is a shorthand (just barely) for `rgba(0,0,0,0)`, which is the computed value any time `transparent` is used.

Number Values

A number value is expressed as a positive or negative number (when permitted). Numbers can be either real (represented as `<number>`) or integers (`<integer>`). They may also restrict the range of acceptable values, as with color values that accept only integers in the range 0–255. A more common range restriction is to limit a number to be non-negative. These are sometimes represented as `<non-negative number>` or `<non-negative integer>`.

Percentage Values

A percentage value is expressed as a `<number>` followed immediately by a percent sign (%). There should never be any space between the number and the percent sign. A percentage value will always be computed relative to something else. For example, declaring `font-size: 120%;` for an element sets its font size to 120% of the computed `font-size` of its parent element. Some properties may restrict the values to be non-negative.

Length Values

A length value is expressed as a positive or negative number (when permitted), followed immediately by a two-letter abbreviation that represents the units to be used. There should never be any space between the number and the unit designator. A value of 0 (zero) does not require a unit designator. Length units are divided into two types: *absolute units*, which are (in theory) always measured in the same way, and *relative units*, which are measured in relation to other things.

Absolute Length Units

Inches (`in`)

> As you might expect, the same inches found on typical US rulers. The mapping from inches to a monitor or other display device is usually approximate at best because many systems have no concept of the relation of their display areas to "real-world" measurements such as inches. Thus, inches should be used with extreme caution in screen design.

Centimeters (`cm`)

> The centimeters found on rulers the world over. There are 2.54 centimeters to an inch, and 1 centimeter equals 0.394 inches. The same mapping warnings that applied to inches also apply to centimeters.

Millimeters (`mm`)

> There are 10 millimeters to a centimeter, so you get 25.4 millimeters to an inch, and 1 millimeter equals 0.0394 inches. Bear in mind the previous warnings about mapping lengths to monitors.

Points (`pt`)

> Points are standard typographical measures used by printers and typesetters for decades and by word-processing programs for many years. By modern definition, there are 72 points to an inch. Therefore, the capital letters of text set to 12 points should be one-sixth of an inch tall. For example, `p {font-size: 18pt;}` is equivalent to `p {font-size: 0.25in;}`, assuming proper mapping of lengths to the display environment (see previous comments).

Picas (`pc`)

> Another typographical term. A pica is equivalent to 12 points, which means there are 6 picas to an inch. The capital letters of text set to 1 pica should be one-sixth of an inch tall. For example, `p {font-size: 1.5pc;}` would set text to be the same size as the example declarations found in the definition of points. Keep in mind previous warnings.

Relative Length Units

Em-height (em)
> This refers to the em-height of a given font. In CSS, the em-height is equivalent to the height of the character box for a given font, which is to say that computed value of `font-size`. Ems can be used to set relative sizes for fonts; for example, `1.2em` is the same as saying `120%`.

Root element em-height (rem)
> This refers to the em-height of the root element (in HTML and XHTML, the `html` element). Otherwise it is the same as `em`.

X-height (ex)
> This refers to the x-height of the font. However, the vast majority of fonts do not include their x-height, so many browsers approximate it (poorly) by simply setting `1ex` to be equal to `0.5em`. The exception is IE5/Mac, which attempts to determine the actual x-height of a font by internally bitmapping a very large "x" and counting pixels!

ZERO width (ch)
> This refers to the width of a single zero (Unicode +0300, "ZERO") in the current font family and size.

Pixels (px)
> A pixel is a small box on screen, but CSS defines pixels more abstractly. In CSS terms, a pixel is defined to be about the size required to yield 96 pixels per inch. Many user agents ignore this definition in favor of simply addressing the pixels on the monitor. Scaling factors are brought into play when page zooming or printing, where an element `100px` wide can be rendered more than 100 device dots wide.

Viewport width unit (vw)
> This unit is calculated with respect to the viewport's width, which is divided by 100. If the viewport is 937 pixels wide, for example, `1vw` is equal to `9.37px`. If the viewport's width changes, say by dragging the browser

window wider or more narrow, the value of **vw** changes along with it.

*Viewport height unit (*vh*)*
> This unit is calculated with respect to the viewport's height, which is divided by 100. If the viewport is 650 pixels tall, for example, **1vh** is equal to **6.5px**. If the viewport's height changes, say by dragging the browser window taller or shorter, the value of **vh** changes along with it.

*Viewport minimum unit (*vm*)*
> This unit is 1/100 of the viewport's width or height, whichever is *lesser*. Thus, given a viewport that is 937 pixels wide by 650 pixels tall, **1vm** is equal to **6.5px**.

URIs

A URI value (**<uri>**) is a reference to a file such as a graphic or another style sheet. CSS defines a URI as relative to the style sheet that contains it. URI stands for Uniform Resource Identifier, which is the more recent name for URLs. (Technically, URLs are a subset of URIs.) In CSS, which was first defined when URIs were still called URLs, this means that references to URIs will actually appear in the form **url(<uri>)**. Fun!

Angles

The format of an **<angle>** is expressed as a **<number>** followed immediately by an angle unit. There are four types of angle units: degrees (**deg**), grads (**grad**), radians (**rad**), and turns (**turn**). For example, a right angle could be declared as **90deg**, **100grad**, **1.571rad**, or **0.25turn**; in each case, the values are translated into degrees in the range 0 through 360. This is also true of negative values, which are allowed. The measure **-90deg** is the same as **270deg**.

Times

A time value (`<time>`) is expressed as a non-negative `<number>` followed immediately by a time unit. There are two types of time units: seconds (`s`) and milliseconds (`ms`). Time values appear in aural styles, which are not widely supported, and in the much better supported transitions and animations.

Frequencies

A frequency value (`<frequency>`) is expressed as a non-negative `<number>` followed immediately by a frequency unit. There are two types of frequency units: hertz (`Hz`) and kilohertz (`kHz`). The unit identifiers are case-insensitive, so `6kHz` and `6khz` are equivalent. As of this writing, frequency values are only used with aural styles, which are not well supported.

Strings

A string (`<string>`) is a series of characters enclosed by either single or double quotes. If a string needs to include the same quote that encloses it, it must be escaped. For example, `'That \'s amazing!'` or `"Deploy the \"scare quotes\" at once!"`. If a newline is needed within a string, it is represented as `\A`, which is the Unicode codepoint for the line feed character. Any Unicode character can be represented using an escaped codepoint reference; thus, a left curly double quotation mark is represented `\201C`. If a string does contain a linefeed for legibility reasons, it must be escaped and will be removed when processing the string.

CHAPTER 3

Selectors

Selectors

Universal Selector

Pattern:

*

Description:

This selector matches any element name in the document's language. If a rule does not have an explicit selector, the universal selector is inferred.

Examples:

```
* {color: red;}
div * p {color: blue;}
```

Type Selector

Pattern:

element1

Description:

This selector matches the name of an element in the document's language. Every instance of the element name is matched. (CSS1 referred to these as "element selectors.")

Examples:

```
body {background: #FFF;}
p {font-size: 1em;}
```

Descendant Selector

Pattern:

```
element1 element2
```

Description:

This allows the author to select an element based on its status as a descendant of another element. The matched element can be a child, grandchild, great-grandchild, etc., of the ancestor element. (CSS1 referred to these as "contextual selectors.")

Examples:

```
body h1 {font-size: 200%;}
table tr td div ul li {color: purple;}
```

Child Selector

Pattern:

```
element1 > element2
```

Description:

This type of selector is used to match an element based on its status as a child of another element. It is more restrictive than a descendant selector, as only a child will be matched.

Examples:

```
div > p {color: cyan;}
ul > li {font-weight: bold;}
```

Adjacent Sibling Selector

Pattern:

```
element1 + element2
```

Description:

This allows the author to select an element that is the following adjacent sibling of another element. (Sibling elements, as the name implies, share the same parent element.) Any text between the two elements is ignored; only elements and their positions in the document tree are considered.

Examples:

```
table + p {margin-top: 2.5em;}
h1 + * {margin-top: 0;}
```

General Sibling Selector

Pattern:

```
element1 ~ element2
```

Description:

This allows the author to select an element that is a sibling of another element and follows it in the document tree. Any text or other elements between the two elements are ignored; only elements and their positions in the document tree are considered.

Examples:

```
h1 ~ h2 {margin-top: 2.5em;}
div#navlinks ~ div {margin-top: 0;}
```

Class Selector

Pattern:

```
element1.classname
element1.classname1.classname2
```

Description:

In languages that permit it, such as HTML, XHTML, SVG, and MathML, a class selector using "dot notation" can be used to select elements that have a class attribute containing a specific value or values. The name of the class value must immediately follow the dot. Multiple class values can be chained together, although there are support problems in Internet Explorer previous to IE7. If no element name precedes the dot, the selector matches all elements bearing that class value or values.

Examples:

```
p.urgent {color: red;}
a.external {font-style: italic;}
.example {background: olive;}
.note.caution {background: yellow;}
```

Note:

Internet Explorer previous to IE7 does not support the chained selector syntax, though it does permit multiple words in class values in the markup.

ID Selector

Pattern:

element1#idname

Description:

In languages that permit it, such as HTML or XHTML, an ID selector using "hash notation" can be used to select elements that have an ID containing a specific value or values. The name of the ID value must immediately follow the octothorpe (#). If no element name precedes the octothorpe, the selector matches all elements containing that ID value.

Examples:

```
h1#page-title {font-size: 250%;}
body#home {background: silver;}
#example {background: lime;}
```

Simple Attribute Selector

Pattern:

element1[attr]

Description:

This allows authors to select any element based on the presence of an attribute, regardless of the attribute's value.

Examples:

```
a[rel] {border-bottom: 3px double gray;}
p[class] {border: 1px dotted silver;}
```

Exact Attribute Value Selector

Pattern:

element1[attr="value"]

Description:

This allows authors to select any element based on the precise and complete value of an attribute.

Examples:

```
a[rel="Start"] {font-weight: bold;}
p[class="urgent"] {color: red;}
```

Partial Attribute Value Selector

Pattern:

element1[attr~="value"]

Description:

This allows authors to select any element based on a portion of the space-separated value of an attribute. Note that [class~="value"] is equivalent to .value (see above).

Examples:

```
a[rel~="friend"] {text-transform: uppercase;}
p[class~="warning"] {background: yellow;}
```

Beginning Substring Attribute Value Selector

Pattern:

```
element1[attr^="substring"]
```

Description:

This allows authors to select any element based on a substring at the very beginning of an attribute's value.

Examples:

```
a[href^="/blog"] {text-transform: uppercase;}
p[class^="test-"] {background: yellow;}
```

Ending Substring Attribute Value Selector

Pattern:

```
element1[attr$="substring"]
```

Description:

This allows authors to select any element based on a substring at the very end of an attribute's value.

Example:

```
a[href$=".pdf"] {font-style: italic;}
```

Arbitrary Substring Attribute Value Selector

Pattern:

```
element1[attr*="substring"]
```

Description:

This allows authors to select any element based on a substring found anywhere within an attribute's value.

Examples:

```
a[href*="oreilly.com"] {font-weight: bold;}
div [class*="port"] {border: 1px solid red;}
```

Language Attribute Selector

Pattern:

```
element1[lang|="lc"]
```

Description:

This allows authors to select any element with a `lang` attribute whose value is a hyphen-separated list of values, starting with the value provided in the selector.

Example:

```
html[lang|="tr"] {color: red;}
```

Structural Pseudo-Classes

Strictly speaking, all pseudo-classes (like all selectors) are structural: they are, after all, dependent on document structure in some fashion. What sets the pseudo-classes listed here apart is that they are intrinsically about patterns found in the structure of the document, like selecting every other paragraph or elements that are the last children of their parent element.

:empty

Applies to:

Any element

Description:

Matches elements that have no child nodes; that is, no child elements *or* content nodes. Content nodes are defined as any text, whitespace, entity reference, or CDATA nodes. Thus, `<p> </p>` is *not* empty; nor is the element empty if the space is replaced with a newline. Note that this pseudo-class does *not* apply to empty elements such as `br`, `img`, `input`, and so on.

Examples:

```
p:empty {padding: 1em; background: red;}
li:empty {display: none;}
```

:first-child

Applies to:

Any element

Description:

Matches an element when it is the first child of another element. Thus, `div:first-child` will select any `div` that is the first child of another element, *not* the first child element of any `div`.

Examples:

```
td:first-child {border-left: 1px solid;}
p:first-child {text-indent: 0; margin-top: 2em;}
```

:first-of-type

Applies to:

Any element

Description:

Matches an element when it is the first child of its type of another element. Thus, `div:first-of-type` will select any `div` that is the first child `div` of another element.

Examples:

```
td:first-of-type {border-left: 1px dotted;}
h2:first-of-type {color: fuchsia;}
```

:lang

Applies to:

Any element with associated language-encoding information.

Description:

This matches elements based on their human-language encoding. Such language information must be contained within or otherwise associated with the document; it cannot be assigned from CSS. The handling of :lang is the same as for |= attribute selectors. For example, in an HTML document, the language of an element is determined by its lang attribute. If the document does not have one, the language of an element is determined by the lang attribute of its nearest ancestor that does have one, and lacking that, by the Content-Language HTTP header response field (or the respective meta http-equiv) for the document.

Examples:

```
html:lang(en) {background: silver;}
*:lang(fr) {quotes: '&#171; ' ' &#187;';}
```

:last-child

Applies to:

Any element

Description:

Matches an element when it is the last child of another element. Thus, div:last-child will select any div that is the last child of another element, *not* the last child element of any div.

Examples:

```
td:last-child {border-right: 1px solid;}
p:last-child {margin-bottom: 2em;}
```

:last-of-type

Applies to:

Any element

Description:

Matches an element when it is the last child of its type of another element. Thus, `div:last-of-type` will select any `div` that is the last child `div` of another element.

Examples:

```
td:last-of-type {border-right: 1px dotted;}
h2:last-of-type {color: fuchsia;}
```

:nth-child(an+b)

Applies to:

Any element

Description:

Matches every nth child with the pattern of selection defined by the formula $an+b$, where a and b are `<integer>`s and n represents an infinite series of integers, counting forward from the first child. Thus, to select every fourth child of the `body` element, starting with the first child, you write `body > *:nth-child(4n+1)`. This will select the first, fifth, ninth, fourteenth, and so on children of the `body`. If you literally wish to select the fourth, eighth, twelfth, and so on children, you would modify the selector to `body > *:nth-child(4n)`. It is also possible to have b be negative, so that `body > *:nth-child(4n-1)` selects the third, seventh, eleventh, fifteenth, and so on children of the `body`.

In place of the $an+b$ formula, there are two keywords permitted: even and odd. These are equivalent to `2n` and `2n+1`, respectively.

Examples:

```
*:nth-child(4n+1) {font-weight: bold;}
tbody tr:nth-child(odd) {background-color: #EEF;}
```

:nth-last-child(an+b)

Applies to:

Any element

Description:

Matches every nth child with the pattern of selection defined by the formula *an+b*, where *a* and *b* are <integer>s and n represents an infinite series of integers, *counting backward from the last child*. Thus, to select every fourth-to-last child of the body element, starting with the last child, you write body > *:nth-last-child(4n+1). This is in effect the mirror image of :nth-child.

In place of the *an+b* formula, there are two keywords permitted: even and odd. These are equivalent to 2n and 2n+1, respectively.

Examples:

```
*:nth-last-child(4n+1) {font-weight: bold;}
tbody tr:nth-last-child(odd) {background-color: #EEF;}
```

:nth-last-of-type(an+b)

Applies to:

Any element

Description:

Matches every nth child that is of the same type as the element named, with the pattern of selection defined by the formula *an+b*, where *a* and *b* are <integer>s and n represents an infinite series of integers, *counting backward from the last such element*. Thus, to select every third-to-last paragraph (p) that is a child of the body element, starting with the first such paragraph, you write body > p:nth-last-of-type(3n+1). This holds true even if other elements are interspersed between the various paragraphs, such as lists, tables, or other elements.

In place of the *an+b* formula, there are two keywords permitted: even and odd. These are equivalent to 2n and 2n+1, respectively.

Examples:

```
td:nth-last-of-type(even) {background-color: #FCC;}
img:nth-last-of-type(3n) {float: left; border: 2px solid;}
```

:nth-of-type(an+b)

Applies to:

Any element

Description:

Matches every nth child that is of the same type as the element named, with the pattern of selection defined by the formula *an+b*, where *a* and *b* are `<integer>`s and n represents an infinite series of integers, counting forward from the first such element. Thus, to select every third paragraph (p) that is a child of the body element, starting with the first such paragraph, you write body > p:nth-of-type(3n+1). This will select the first, fourth, seventh, tenth, and so on child paragraphs of the body. This holds true even if other elements are interspersed between the various paragraphs, such as lists, tables, or other elements.

In place of the *an+b* formula, there are two keywords permitted: even and odd. These are equivalent to 2n and 2n+1, respectively.

Examples:

```
td:nth-of-type(even) {background-color: #FCC;}
img:nth-of-type(3n) {float: right; margin-left: 1em;}
```

:only-child

Applies to:

Any element

Description:

Matches an element that is the only child element of its parent element. A common use case for this selector is to remove the border from any linked image, assuming that said image is the only element in the link. Note that an element can be selected by :only-child even if it has its own child or children. It must only be the only child of its parent.

Examples:

```
a img:only-child {border: 0;}
table div:only-child {margin: 5px;}
```

:only-of-type

Applies to:

Any element

Description:

Matches an element that is the only child element of its type to its parent element. Note that an element can be selected by :only-of-type even if it has its own child or children of its own type (such as divs within a div). It must only be the only child of its type to its parent.

Examples:

```
p em:only-of-type {font-weight: bold;}
section article:only-of-type {margin: 2em 0 3em;}
```

:root

Applies to:

The root element

Description:

This matches the document's root element, which in HTML and XHTML is always the html element. In XML formats, the root element can have any name; thus, a generic root-element selector is needed.

Examples:

```
:root {font: medium serif;}
:root > * {margin: 1.5em 0;}
```

The Negation Pseudo-Class

There is but one pseudo-class that handles negation, but it is so unique that it deserves its own subsection.

:not(e)

Applies to:

Any element

Description:

Matches every element that is *not* described by the simple selector *e*. This allows authors to select, say, every element that is not a paragraph by stating `*:not(p)`. More usefully, negation can be used within the context of descendant selectors. An example of this would be selecting every element within a table that was not a data cell using `table *:not(td)`. Another example would be selecting every element with an ID that was not "search" by using `[id]:not([id="search"])`.

Note that there is one exception to the "simple selector" definition of *e*: it cannot be a negation pseudo-class. That is, it is impermissible to write `:not(:not(div))`. This is no great loss, since the equivalent of that would be `div`.

Because `:not()` is a pseudo-class, it can be chained with other pseudo-classes as well as with instances of itself. For example, to select any focused element that isn't an `a` element, use `*:focus:not(a)`. To select any element that isn't either a paragraph or a div, use `*:not(p):not(div)`.

As of mid-2011, the "simple selector" restriction means that grouped and descendant selectors are not permitted within `:not()` expressions. This restriction is likely to be loosened or eliminated in future versions of the CSS Selectors module.

Examples:

```
ul *:not(li) {text-indent: 2em;}
fieldset *:not([type="checkbox"]):not([type="radio"])
   {margin: 0 1em;}
```

Interaction Pseudo-Classes

The pseudo-classes listed here are all related to the user's interaction with the document: whether styling different link states, highlighting an element that's the target of a fragment identifier, or styling form elements based on their being enabled or disabled.

:active

Applies to:

An element that is being activated

Description:

This applies to an element during the period in which it is being activated. The most common example is clicking on a hyperlink in an HTML document: while the mouse button is being held down, the link is active. There are other ways to activate elements, and other elements can in theory be activated, although CSS doesn't define them.

Examples:

```
a:active {color: red;}
*:active {background: blue;}
```

:checked

Applies to:

Any element

Description:

Matches any user interface element that has been "toggled on," such as a checked checkbox or a filled radio button.

Examples:

```
input:checked {outline: 3px solid rgba(127,127,127,0.5);}
input[type="checkbox"]:checked {box-shadow: red 0 0 5px;}
```

:disabled

Applies to:

Any element

Description:

Matches user interface elements that are not able to accept user input because of language attributes or other nonpresentational means; for example, `<input type="text" disabled>` in HTML5. Note that `:disabled` does *not* apply when an `input` element has simply been removed from the viewport with properties like `position` or `display`.

Examples:

```
input:disabled {opacity: 0.5;}
```

:enabled

Applies to:

Any element

Description:

Matches user interface elements that are able to accept user input and that can be set to "enabled" and "disabled" states through the markup language itself. This includes any form input element in (X)HTML, but does not include hyperlinks.

Examples:

```
input:enabled {background: #FCC;}
```

:focus

Applies to:

An element that has focus

Description:

This applies to an element during the period in which it has focus. One example from HTML is an input box that has the text-input cursor within it such that when the user starts typing, text will be entered into that box. Other elements, such as hyperlinks, can also have focus; however, CSS does not define which elements may have focus.

Examples:

```
a:focus {outline: 1px dotted red;}
input:focus {background: yellow;}
```

Note:

:focus support in Internet Explorer applies only to hyperlinks and does not extend to form controls.

:hover

Applies to:

An element that is in a hovered state

Description:

This applies to an element during the period in which it is being *hovered* (when the user is designating an element without activating it). The most common example of this is moving the mouse pointer inside the boundaries of a hyperlink in an HTML document. Other elements can in theory be hovered, although CSS doesn't define which ones.

Examples:

```
a[href]:hover {text-decoration: underline;}
p:hover {background: yellow;}
```

Note:

:hover support in Internet Explorer applies only to hyperlinks in versions previous to IE7.

:link

Applies to:

A hyperlink to another resource that has not been visited

Description:

This applies to a link to a URI that has not been visited; that is, the URI to which the link points does not appear in the user agent's history. This state is mutually exclusive with the :visited state.

Examples:

```
a:link {color: blue;}
*:link {text-decoration: underline;}
```

:target

Applies to:

Any element

Description:

Matches an element which is itself matched by the fragment identifier portion of the URI used to access the page. Thus, http://www.w3.org/TR/css3-selectors/#target-pseudo would be matched by :target and would apply the declared styles to any element with the id of target-pseudo. If that element was a paragraph, it would also be matched by p:target.

Examples:

```
:target {background: #EE0;}
```

:visited

Applies to:

A hyperlink to another resource that has already been visited

Description:

This applies to a link to a URI that has been visited; that is, the URI to which the link points appears in the user agent's history. This state is mutually exclusive with the :link state.

Examples:

```
a:visited {color: purple;}
*:visited {color: gray;}
```

Pseudo-Elements

In CSS1 and CSS2, pseudo-elements were preceded by single colons, just as pseudo-classes were. In CSS3, pseudo-elements use double colons to distinguish them from pseudo-classes. For historical reasons, browsers will support both single- and double-colons on pseudo-elements, but the double-colon syntax is recommended.

::after

Generates:

A pseudo-element containing generated content placed after the content in the element

Description:

This allows the author to insert generated content at the end of an element's content. By default, the pseudo-element is inline, but it can be changed using the property display.

Examples:

```
a.external:after {content: " " url(/icons/globe.gif);}
p:after {content: " | ";}
```

::before

Generates:

A pseudo-element containing generated content placed before the content in the element

Description:

This allows the author to insert generated content at the beginning of an element's content. By default, the pseudo-element is inline, but that can be changed using the property display.

Examples:

```
a[href]:before {content: "[LINK] ";)
p:before {content: attr(class);}
a[rel|="met"]:after {content: " *";}
```

::first-letter

Generates:

A pseudo-element that contains the first letter of an element

Description:

This is used to style the first letter of an element. Any leading punctuation should be styled along with the first letter. Some languages have letter combinations that should be treated as a single character, and a user agent may apply the first letter style to both. Prior to CSS2.1, :first-letter could be attached only to block-level elements. CSS2.1 expanded its scope to include block, list-item, table-call, table caption, and inline-block elements. There is a limited set of properties that can apply to a first letter.

Examples:

```
h1:first-letter {font-size: 166%;}
p:first-letter {text-decoration: underline;}
```

::first-line

Generates:

A pseudo-element that contains the first formatted line of an element

Description:

This is used to style the first line of text in an element, regardless of how many or how few words may appear in that line. :first-line can be attached only to block-level elements. There is a limited set of properties that can apply to a first line.

Example:

```
p.lead:first-line {font-weight: bold;}
```

Media Queries

With media queries, an author can define the media environment in which a given style sheet is used by the browser. In the past, this was handled by setting media types with the `media` attribute on `link` elements or the media descriptor on `@import` declarations. Media queries take this concept several steps further by allowing authors to choose style sheets based on the features of a given media type.

Basic Concepts

The placement of media queries will be very familiar to any author who has ever set a media type. Here are two ways of applying an external style sheet when rendering the document on a color printer:

```
<link href="print-color.css" type="text/css"
    media="print and (color)" rel="stylesheet">

@import url(print-color.css) print and (color);
```

Anywhere a media type can be used, a media query can be used. This means that it is possible to list more than one query in a comma-separated list:

```
<link href="print-color.css" type="text/css"
    media="print and (color), projection and (color)"
    rel="stylesheet">

@import url(print-color.css) print and (color),
    projection and (color);
```

In any situation where one of the media queries evaluates to "true," the associated style sheet is applied. Thus, given the previous @import, print-color.css will be applied if rendering to a color printer or a color projection environment. If printing on a black-and-white printer, both queries will evaluate to "false" and print-color.css will not be applied to the document. The same holds for any screen medium, a grayscale projection environment, an aural media environment, and so forth.

Each query is composed of a media type and one or more listed media features. Each media feature is enclosed in parentheses, and multiple features are linked with the **and** keyword. There are two logical keywords in media queries:

and

> Links together two or more media features in such a way that all of them must be true for the query to be true. For example, (color) and (orientation: landscape) and (min-device-width: 800px) means that all three conditions must be satisfied: if the media environment has color, is in landscape orientation, and the device's display is at least 800 pixels wide, the style sheet is used.

not

> Negates the entire query so that if all of the conditions are true, the style sheet is *not* applied. For example, not (color) and (orientation: landscape) and (min-device-width: 800px) means that if the three conditions are satisfied, the statement is negated. Thus, if the media environment has color, is in landscape orientation, and the

device's display is at least 800 pixels wide, the style sheet is *not* used. In all other cases, it will be used. Note that the `not` keyword can only be used at the beginning of a media query. It is *not* legal to write something like `(color) and not (mid-device-width: 800px)`. In such cases, the query will be ignored. Note also that browsers too old to understand media queries will always skip a style sheet whose media descriptor starts with `not`.

There is no *or* keyword for use within a given query. The commas that separate a list of queries do serve the function of an or—`screen, print` means "apply if the media is screen or print." Thus, instead of `screen and (max-color: 2) or (mono chrome)`, which is invalid and thus ignored, you should write `screen and (max-color: 2), screen and (monochrome)`.

There is one more keyword, `only`, which is designed to create deliberate backward incompatibility.

`only`

> Used to hide a style sheet from browsers too old to understand media queries. For example, to apply a style sheet in all media, but only in those browsers that understand media queries, you write something like `@import url(new.css) only all`. In browsers that do understand media queries, the `only` keyword is ignored. Note that the `only` keyword can only be used at the beginning of a media query.

Media Query Values

There are two new value types introduced by media queries, which (as of early 2011) are not used in any other context.

<ratio>

> A ratio value is two positive <integer> values separated by a solidus (/) and optional whitespace. The first value refers to the width, and the second to the height. Thus, to express a width-to-height ratio of 16:9, you can write `16/9` or `16 / 9`.

<resolution>

A resolution value is a positive <integer> followed by either of the unit identifiers `dpi` or `dpcm`. As usual, whitespace is not permitted between the <integer> and the identifier.

Media Features

Note that none of the following values can be negative.

`width, min-width, max-width`
Values: <length>

Refers to the width of the display area of the user agent. In a screen-media web browser, this is the width of the viewport plus any scrollbars. In paged media, this is the width of the page box. Thus, (`min-width: 850px`) applies when the viewport is greater than 850 pixels wide.

`device-width, min-device-width, max-device-width`
Values: <length>

Refers to the width of the complete rendering area of the output device. In screen media, this is the width of the screen. In paged media, this is the width of the page. Thus, (`max-device-width: 1200px`) applies when the device's output area is less than 1200 pixels wide.

`height, min-height, max-height`
Values: <length>

Refers to the height of the display area of the user agent. In a screen-media web browser, this is the height of the viewport plus any scrollbars. In paged media, this is the height of the page box. Thus, (`height: 567px`) applies when the viewport's height is precisely 567 pixels tall.

`device-height, min-device-height, max-device-height`
Values: <length>

Refers to the height of the complete rendering area of the output device. In screen media, this is the height of the screen. In paged media, this is the height of the page. Thus, (`max-device-height: 400px`) applies when the device's output area is less than 400 pixels tall.

aspect-ratio, min-aspect-ratio, max-aspect-ratio
Values: <ratio>

> Refers to the ratio that results from comparing the width media feature to the height media feature (see the definition of <ratio>). Thus, (min-aspect-ratio: 2/1) applies to any viewport whose width-to-height ratio is at least 2:1.

device-aspect-ratio, min-device-aspect-ratio, max-device-aspect-ratio
Values: <length>

> Refers to the ratio that results from comparing the device-width media feature to the device-eight media feature (see the definition of <ratio>). Thus, (device-aspect-ratio: 16/9) applies to any output device whose display area width-to-height is exactly 16:9.

color, min-color, max-color
Values: <integer>

> Refers to the presence of color-display capability in the output device, with an optional number representing the number of bits used in each color component. Thus, (color) applies to any device with any color depth at all, whereas (min-color: 4) means there must be at least four bits used per color component. Any device that does not support color will return 0.

color-index, min-color-index, max-color-index
Values: <integer>

> Refers to the total number of colors available in the output device's color lookup table. Any device that does not use a color lookup table will return 0. Thus, (min-color-index: 256) applies to any device with a minimum of 256 colors available.

monochrome, min-monochrome, max-monochrome
Values: <integer>

> Refers to the presence of a monochrome display, with an optional number of bits-per-pixel in the output device's frame buffer. Any device that is not monochrome will return 0. Thus, (monochrome) applies to any monochrome output device, whereas (min-monochrome: 2) means any

monochrome output device with a minimum of 2 bits per pixel in the frame buffer.

`resolution`, `min-resolution`, `max-resolution`
Values: <*resolution*>

Refers to the resolution of the output device in terms of pixel density, measured in either dots-per-inch (`dpi`) or dots-per-centimeter (`dpcm`). If an output device has pixels that are not square, the least dense axis is used; for example, if a device is 100dpcm along one axis and 120dpcm along the other, `100` is the value returned. Additionally, a bare `resolution` feature query can never match (though `min-resolution` and `max-resolution` can).

`orientation`
Values: `portrait` | `landscape`

Refers to the output device's total output area, where `portrait` is returned if the media feature `height` is equal to or greater than the media feature `width`. Otherwise, the result is `landscape`.

`scan`
Values: `progressive` | `interlace`

Refers to the scanning process used in an output device with a media type of `tv`.

`grid`
Values: `0` | `1`

Refers to the presence (or absence) of a grid-based output device, such as a `tty` terminal. A grid-based device will return `1`; otherwise, `0` is returned.

CHAPTER 4

Property Reference

Universal Values

Any user agent that has fully implemented the "cascading and inheritance" module will honor the values `inherit` and `initial` on all properties. In practice (as of mid-2011), support for `inherit` is much more widespread than `initial`.

`inherit`

> Forces the value for the property to be inherited from the element's parent element, even if the property in question is not inherited (e.g., `background-image`). Another way to think of this is that the value is copied from the parent element.

`initial`

> Forces the value of the property to be the initial value defined by the relevant CSS module. For example, `font-style: initial` sets the value of `font-style` to `normal` regardless of the `font-style` value that would have been inherited from the parent element. In cases where the initial value is defined as determined by the user agent, such as `font-size`, the value is set to the "default" defined by the user agent's preferences.

Visual Media

animation

Values:

[<animation-parameters>] [, [<animation-parameters>]]*

Expansions:

<animation-parameters>

<'animation-name'> || <'animation-duration'> || <'animation-timing-function'> || <'animation-delay'> || <'animation-iteration-count'> || <'animation-direction'>

Initial value:

Refer to individual properties

Applies to:

Block-level and inline-level elements

Inherited:

No

Computed value:

Same as declared value

Description:

A shorthand property encompassing all the aspects of one or more comma-separated CSS animations. The parts of the value can occur in any order. As a result, beware possible ambiguity in the delay and duration values. As of this writing, it is most likely that the first time value will be taken to define the duration and the second to define the delay, but this cannot be guaranteed.

Examples:

```
div#slide {animation: 'slide' 2.5s linear 0 1 normal;}
h1 {animation: 'bounce' 0.5s 0.33s
    ease-in-out infinite alternate;}
```

animation-delay

Values:

<time> [, <time>]*

Initial value:

0ms

Applies to:

Block-level and inline-level elements

Inherited:

No

Computed value:

Same as declared value

Description:

Defines the amount of time that the user agent waits before starting the CSS animation(s). The timer starts when the UA applies the animation CSS. For a noninteractive element, this is likely (but not guaranteed) to be at the end of page load.

Examples:

```
body {animation-delay: 1s, 2000ms, 4s;}
a:hover {animation-delay: 400ms;}
```

Note:

As of mid-2011, the actual default value in the specification is 0. It is given as 0ms here for clarity's sake, as only length values and numbers are permitted unitless zeroes.

animation-direction

Values:

normal | alternate [, normal | alternate]*

Initial value:

normal

Applies to:

Block-level and inline-level elements

Inherited:

No

Computed value:

Same as declared value

Description:

Specifies whether a CSS animation with more than one cycle (see `animation-iteration-count`) should always go the same direction or should reverse direction on every other cycle. For example, an `alternate` animation that moves an element 300 pixels to the right would move it 300 pixels to the left on every other cycle, thus returning it to its starting position. Setting that same animation to `normal` would cause the element to move 300 pixels right, then jump back to its starting place and move 300 pixels right again, and over and over until the animation stops (assuming it ever does).

Examples:

```
body {animation-direction: alternate, normal, normal;}
#scanner {animation-direction: normal;}
```

animation-duration

Values:

<time> [, <time>]*

Initial value:

0ms

Applies to:

Block-level and inline-level elements

Inherited:

No

Computed value:

Same as declared value

Description:

Defines the length of time it should take for each cycle of a CSS animation to run from start to finish. Therefore, in animations with only one cycle, it defines the total time of the animation. The default value, 0ms, means that there will be no animation besides moving the element from its start state to its end state. Negative values are converted to 0ms.

Examples:

```
h1 {animation-duration: 10s, 5s, 2.5s, 1250ms;}
.zip {animation-duration: 90ms;}
```

Note:

As of mid-2011, the actual default value in the specification is 0. It is given as 0ms here for clarity's sake, as only length values and numbers are permitted unitless zeroes.

animation-iteration-count

Values:

infinite | <number> [, infinite | <number>]*

Initial value:

1

Applies to:

Block-level and inline-level elements

Inherited:

No

Computed value:

Same as declared value

Description:

Defines the number of cycles in the animation(s). The initial value, 1, means that the animation will run exactly once, going from the start state to the end state. A fractional value (e.g., 2.75) means the animation will be halted midway through its final cycle. A value of 0 means that there will be no animation; negative values are converted to 0. As its name implies, infinite means the animation will never end. Use with caution.

Examples:

```
body {animation-iteration-count: 2, 1, 7.5875;}
ol.dance {animation-iteration-count: infinite;}
```

---

animation-name

Values:

none | IDENT [, none | IDENT]*

Initial value:

Applies to:

Block-level and inline-level elements

Inherited:

No

Computed value:

Same as declared value

Description:

Defines the declared name(s) of CSS animation(s). Each IDENT refers to a CSS animation keyframe at-rule. If an IDENT has not been declared or the keyword none is supplied, the animation is not run regardless of the values of any other animation properties. For example, given `animation-name: 'bounce', none, 'jumper';` and that the animation name `jumper` has not been defined, the first animation will run but the second and third will not.

Examples:

```
html {animation-name: 'turn', 'slide', none;}
h2 {animation-name: 'flip';}
```

animation-play-state

Values:

running | paused [, running | paused]*

Initial value:

running

Applies to:

Block-level and inline-level elements

Inherited:

No

Computed value:

Same as declared value

Description:

Defines the run state of one or more CSS animations. The default state of running is the most useful in static CSS environments, but it can be used to easily stop or start animations via DOM scripting or interactive CSS (e.g., :hover).

Examples:

```
pre {animation-play-state: running, paused, running;}
table {animation-play-state: running;}
```

Note:

As of mid-2011, this property was being considered for removal from the CSS Animations Module.

animation-timing-function

Values:

<timing-function> [, < timing-function >]*

Expansions:

<timing-function>

ease | linear | ease-in | ease-out | ease-in-out | cubic-bezier(<number>, <number>, <number>, <number>)

Initial value:

ease

Applies to:

Block-level and inline-level elements

Inherited:

No

Computed value:

Same as declared value

Description:

Defines how an animation is run over the course of an animation's full cycle or within an individual keyframe, depending on where the property is used. The keywords are all defined to have cubic-bezier() equivalents; for example, linear is equivalent to cubic-bezier(0,0,1,1). They should therefore have consistent effects across user agents, though, as always, authors are cautioned to avoid dependency on consistency.

Examples:

```
h1 {animation-timing-function:
    ease, ease-in, cubic-bezier(0.13,0.42,0.67,0.75)}
p {animation-timing-function: linear;}
```

backface-visibility

Values:

visible | hidden

Initial value:

visible

Applies to:

Block-level and inline-level elements

Inherited:

No

Computed value:

Same as declared value

Description:

Defines whether the back side of an element is visible once the element has been rotated in a simulated 3D space and is "facing away" from the viewer. If the value is hidden, the element will be effectively invisible until it is rotated such that the front side of the element is once more "facing toward" the viewer.

Examples:

```
div.card {backface-visibility: hidden;}
span.cubeside {backface-visibility: visible;}
```

background

Values:

[<bg-layer> ,]* <final-bg-layer>

Expansions:

<bg-layer>

<bg-image> || <bg-position> [/ <bg-size>]? || <bg-repeat> || <bg-attachment'> || < bg-box>{1,2}

\<final-bg-layer\>

\<bg-image\> || \<bg-position\> [/ \<bg-size\>]? || \<bg-repeat\> || \<bg-attachment'\> || \< bg-box\>{1,2} || \<bg-color\>

Initial value:

Refer to individual properties

Applies to:

All elements

Inherited:

No

Percentages:

Allowed for \<bg-position\> (see `background-position`) and refer to both the dimensions of the element's background area and the dimensions of the origin image

Computed value:

See individual properties

Description:

A shorthand way of expressing the various background properties of one or more element backgrounds using a single declaration. As with all shorthands, this property will set all of the allowed values (e.g., the repeat, position, and so on) to their defaults if the values are not explicitly supplied. Thus, the following two rules will have the same appearance:

```
background: yellow;
background: yellow none top left repeat;
```

Furthermore, these defaults can override previous declarations made with more specific background properties. For example, given the following rules:

```
h1 {background-repeat: repeat-x;}
h1, h2 {background: yellow url(headback.gif);}
```

...the repeat value for both h1 and h2 elements will be set to the default of repeat, overriding the previously declared value of repeat-x.

When declaring multiple backgrounds, only the last may have a background color. In cases where multiple background images overlap, the images are stacked with the first highest and the last lowest. This is the exact reverse of how overlapping is handled in CSS positioning, and so may seem counterintuitive.

Examples:

```
body {background: white url(bg41.gif)
    fixed center repeat-x;}
p {background:
    url(/pix/water.png) center repeat-x,
    top left url(/pix/stone.png) #555;}
pre {background: yellow;}
```

---

background-attachment

Values:

<bg-attachment> [, <bg-attachment>]*

Expansions:

<bg-attachment>

scroll | fixed | local

Initial value:

scroll

Applies to:

All elements

Inherited:

No

Computed value:

Same as declared value

Description:

Defines whether background images scroll along with the element when the document is scrolled. This property can be used to create

---

"aligned" backgrounds; for more details, see Chapter 9 of *CSS: The Definitive Guide*, third edition (O'Reilly).

Examples:

```
body {background-attachment: scroll, scroll, fixed;}
div.fixbg {background-attachment: fixed;}
```

Note:

In versions of Internet Explorer before IE7, this property is supported only for the body element.

background-clip

Values:

<bg-box> [, <bg-box>]*

Expansions:

<bg-box>

border-box | padding-box | content-box

Initial value:

border-box

Applies to:

All elements

Inherited:

No

Computed value:

Same as declared value

Description:

Defines the boundary within the element box at which the background is clipped; that is, no longer drawn. Historically, this has been equivalent to the default value of border-box, where the background goes to the outer edge of the border area. This property allows more constrained clipping boxes at the outer edge of the padding area and at the content edge itself.

Examples:

```
body {background-clip: content-box;}
.callout {
    background-clip: content-box, border-box,
    padding-box;}
```

---

background-color

Values:

<color>

Initial value:

transparent

Applies to:

All elements

Inherited:

No

Computed value:

Same as declared value

Description:

Defines a solid color for the background of the element. This color fills the box defined by the value of background-clip—by default, the content, padding, and border areas of the element, extending to the outer edge of the element's border. Borders that have transparent sections (such as dashed borders) will show the background color through the transparent sections in cases where the background color extends into the border area.

Examples:

```
h4 {background-color: white;}
p {background-color: rgba(50%,50%,50%,0.33);}
pre {background-color: #FF9;}
```

---

background-image

Values:

<bg-image> [, <bg-image>]*

Expansions:

<bg-image>

| none

Initial value:

Applies to:

All elements

Inherited:

No

Computed value:

Absolute URI

Description:

Places one or more images in the background of the element. Depending on the value of background-repeat, the image may tile infinitely, along one axis, or not at all. The initial background image (the origin image) is placed according to the value of background-position.

Examples:

```
body {
     background-image: url(bg41.gif), url(bg43.png),
     url(bg51.jpg);}
h2 {background-image: url(http://www.pix.org/dots.png);}
```

background-origin

Values:

<bg-box> [, <bg-box>]*

Expansions:

\<bg-box\>

border-box | padding-box | content-box

Initial value:

padding-box

Applies to:

All elements

Inherited:

No

Computed value:

Same as declared value

Description:

Defines the boundary within the element box against which background-image positioning is calculated. Historically, this has been equivalent to the default value of padding-box. This property allows for different positioning contexts. Note that if the value of background-origin is "further out" than the value for background-clip, and the image is positioned to an edge, part of it may be clipped. For example:

```
div#example {background-origin: border-box;
    background-clip: content-box;
    background-position: 100% 100%;}
```

In this case the image will be placed so that its bottom-right corner aligns with the bottom-right corner of the outer border edge, but the only parts of it that will be visible are those that fall within the content area.

Examples:

```
html, body {background-origin: border-box;}
h1 {background-origin: content-box, padding-box;}
```

background-position

Values:

<bg-position> [, <bg-position>]*

Expansions:

<bg-position>

[[top | bottom]] | [<percentage> | <length> | left | center |
right] [<percentage> | <length> | top | center | bottom]? |
[center | [left | right] [<percentage> | <length>]?] &&
[center | [top | bottom] [<percentage> | <length>]?]]

Initial value:

0% 0%

Applies to:

All elements

Inherited:

No

Percentages:

Refer to the corresponding point on both the element and the origin
image

Computed value:

The absolute length offsets if <length> is declared; otherwise, percentage values

Description:

Defines the position(s) of one or more backgrounds' origin images
(as defined by background-image); this is the point from which any
background repetition or tiling will occur. Percentage values define
not only a point within the element, but also the same point in the
origin image itself, thus allowing (for example) an image to be centered by declaring its position to be 50% 50%. When percentage or
length values are used, the first is always the horizontal position,
and the second the vertical. If only one value is given, it sets the
horizontal position, while the missing value is assumed to be either

center or 50%. Negative values are permitted and may place the origin image outside the element's content area without actually rendering it. The context within which an origin image is placed can be affected by the value of background-origin.

Examples:

```
body {background-position: top center;}
div#navbar {background-position: right, 50% 75%, 0 40px;}
pre {background-position: 10px 50%;}
```

background-repeat

Values:

<bg-repeat-style> [, <bg-repeat-style>]*

Expansions:

<bg-repeat-style>

repeat-x | repeat-y | [repeat | space | round | no-repeat]{1,2}

Initial value:

repeat

Applies to:

All elements

Inherited:

No

Computed value:

Same as declared value

Description:

Defines the tiling pattern for one or more background images. The repetition begins from the origin image, which is defined as the value of background-image and is placed according to the value of background-position (and possibly background-origin). For the keywords space and round, the image is tiled as many times as it will fit in the background area without being clipped and then the first and last images are placed against their respective background edges. The difference is that space causes the intervening images to be regularly spaced, and round causes them to be stretched to touch each other. Note that repeat-x is equivalent to repeat no-repeat, and repeat-y is equivalent to no-repeat repeat.

Examples:

```
body {background-repeat: no-repeat;}
h2 {background-repeat: repeat-x, repeat-y, space;}
ul {background-repeat: repeat-y, round space, repeat;}
```

background-size

Values:

<bg-size> [, <bg-size>]*

Expansions:

<bg-repeat-style>

[<length> | <percentage> | auto]{1,2} | cover | contain

Initial value:

auto

Applies to:

All elements

Inherited:

No

Computed value:

See description

Description:

Defines the size of one or more background origin images. If two keywords are used (e.g., 50px 25%), the first defines the horizontal size of the image and the second defines the vertical size. The origin image can be deformed to exactly cover the background with 100% 100%. By contrast, cover scales up the image to cover the entire

---

background even if some of it exceeds the background area and is thus clipped, and `contain` scales up the origin image so that at least one of its dimensions exactly fills the corresponding axis of the background area.

Examples:

```
body {background-size: 100% 90%;}
div.photo {background-size: cover;}
```

border

Values:

<'border-width'> || <'border-style'> || <color>

Initial value:

Refer to individual properties

Applies to:

All elements

Inherited:

No

Computed value:

Same as declared value

Description:

A shorthand property that defines the width, color, and style of an element's border. Note that while none of the values are actually required, omitting a border style will result in no border being applied because the default border style is `none`.

Examples:

```
h1 {border: 2px dashed olive;}
a:link {border: blue solid 1px;}
p.warning {border: double 5px red;}
```

border-bottom

Values:

<'border-width'> || <'border-style'> || <color>

Initial value:

Not defined for shorthand properties

Applies to:

All elements

Inherited:

No

Computed value:

See individual properties

Description:

A shorthand property that defines the width, color, and style of the bottom border of an element. As with border, omission of a border style will result in no border appearing.

Examples:

```
ul {border-bottom: 0.5in groove green;}
a:active {border-bottom: purple 2px dashed;}
```

border-bottom-color

Values:

<color>

Initial value:

The value of color for the element

Applies to:

All elements

Inherited:

No

Computed value:

If no value is declared, use the computed value of the property color for the same element; otherwise, same as declared value

Description:

Defines the color for the visible portions of the bottom border of an element. The border's style must be something other than none or hidden for any visible border to appear.

Examples:

```
ul {border-bottom-color: green;}
a:active {border-bottom-color: purple;}
```

border-bottom-left-radius

Values:

[<length> | <percentage>] [<length> | <percentage>]?

Initial value:

0

Applies to:

All elements

Inherited:

No

Percentages:

Refer to the dimensions of the element's border box

Computed value:

Same as declared value

Description:

Defines the rounding radius for the bottom-left corner of an element's border. If two values are supplied, the first is the horizontal radius and the second is the vertical radius. See `border-radius` for a description of how the values create the rounding shape.

Examples:

```
h1 {border-bottom-left-radius: 10%;}
h2 {border-bottom-left-radius: 1em 10px;}
```

border-bottom-right-radius

Values:

[<length> | <percentage>] [<length> | <percentage>]?

Initial value:

0

Applies to:

All elements

Inherited:

No

Percentages:

Refer to the dimensions of the element's border box

Computed value:

Same as declared value

Description:

Defines the rounding radius for the bottom-right corner of an element's border. If two values are supplied, the first is the horizontal radius and the second is the vertical radius. See `border-radius` for a description of how the values create the rounding shape.

Examples:

```
h1 {border-bottom-right-radius: 10%;}
h2 {border-bottom-right-radius: 1em 10px;}
```

border-bottom-style

Values:

none | hidden | dotted | dashed | solid | double | groove | ridge |
inset | outset

Initial value:

Applies to:

All elements

Inherited:

No

Computed value:

Same as declared value

Description:

Defines the style for the bottom border of an element. The value
must be something other than none for any border to appear.

Examples:

```
ul {border-bottom-style: groove;}
a:active {border-bottom-style: dashed;}
```

border-bottom-width

Values:

thin | medium | thick | <length>

Initial value:

Applies to:

All elements

Inherited:

No

Computed value:

Absolute length; 0 if the style of the border is none or hidden

Description:

Defines the width for the bottom border of an element, which will take effect only if the border's style is something other than none. If the border style is none, the border width is effectively reset to 0. Negative length values are not permitted.

Examples:

```
ul {border-bottom-width: 0.5in;}
a:active {border-bottom-width: 2px;}
```

border-collapse

Values:

collapse | separate

Initial value:

separate

Applies to:

Elements with a display value of table or inline-table

Inherited:

Yes

Computed value:

Same as declared value

Description:

Defines the layout model used in laying out the borders in a table—i.e., those applied to cells, rows, and so forth. Although the property applies only to tables, it is inherited by all the elements within the table and actually used by them.

Examples:

```
table {border-collapse: separate; border-spacing: 3px 5px;}
```

Note:

In CSS2.0, the default value was `collapse`.

---

border-color

Values:

<color>{1,4}

Initial value:

Not defined for shorthand properties

Applies to:

All elements

Inherited:

No

Computed value:

See individual properties

Description:

A shorthand property that sets the color for the visible portions of the overall border of an element or sets a different color for each of the four sides. Remember that a border's style must be something other than `none` or `hidden` for any visible border to appear.

Examples:

```
h1 {border-color: purple;}
a:visited {border-color: maroon;}
```

---

border-image

Values:

<'border-image-source'> || <'border-image-slice'> [/ <'border-image-width'>? [/ <'border-image-outset'>]?]? || <'border-image-repeat'>

Initial value:

See individual properties

Applies to:

All elements *except* table elements where `border-collapse` is collapse

Inherited:

No

Computed value:

See individual properties

Description:

A shorthand property that defines the source, slicing pattern, border width, degree of extension, and repetition of an image-based border. The syntax is somewhat unusual compared to the rest of CSS, so take extra time with it. For example, three of the five values possible are slash-separated and must be listed in a specific order.

Note that it is effectively impossible to take a simple image (say, a star) and repeat it around the edges of an element. To create that effect, you must create a single image that contains nine copies of the image you wish to repeat in a 3×3 grid. It may also be necessary to set `border-width` (*not* `border-image-width`) to be large enough to show the image, depending on the value of `border-image-outset`.

Examples:

```
div.starry {border-image: url(stargrid.png) 5px repeat;}
aside {
    border-image: url(asides.png) 100 50 150 / 8 3 13 /
    2 stretch round;}
```

Note:

As of early 2011, browser support for border-image was incomplete and inconsistent, whereas none of the related properties (e.g., border-image-source) were supported at all. They are included because browsers were expected to harmonize support by the end of 2011.

border-image-outset

Values:

[<length> | <number>]{1,4}

Initial value:

0

Applies to:

All elements *except* table elements where border-collapse is collapse

Inherited:

No

Computed value:

Same as declared value (but see description)

Description:

Defines the distance by which a border image may exceed the border area of the element. The values define distances from the top, right, bottom, and left edges of the border image, in that order. Numbers are calculated with respect to the image's intrinsic coordinate system; thus, for a raster image, the number 7 is taken to mean seven pixels. Images in formats such as SVG may have different coordinate systems. Negative values are not permitted.

Examples:

```
aside {border-image-outset: 2;}
div#pow {border-image-outset: 10 17 13 5;}
```

Note:

As of early 2011, browsers did not support `border-image-outset`. It is included because `border-image` (which encompasses `border-image-outset`) *was* supported and browsers were expected to add `border-image-outset` support by the end of 2011.

border-image-repeat

Values:

[stretch | repeat | round]{1,2}

Initial value:

stretch

Applies to:

All elements *except* table elements where `border-collapse` is collapse

Inherited:

No

Computed value:

Same as declared value

Description:

Defines the repetition pattern (or lack thereof) of the sides of a border image. `stretch` causes a single copy of the image to be stretched to fit the border segment (top, right, bottom, or left). `repeat` "tiles" the image in a manner familiar from background images, though border images are only ever tiled along one axis. `round` "tiles" the border image as many times as it will fit without clipping, then (if necessary) scales the entire set of tiled images to exactly fit the border segment.

Examples:

```
div.starry {border-image-repeat: repeat;}
aside {border-image-repeat: stretch round;}
```

border-image-slice

Values:

[<number> | <percentage>]{1,4} `&&` `fill?`

Initial value:

100%

Applies to:

All elements *except* table elements where `border-collapse` is `collapse`

Inherited:

No

Percentages:

Refer to the size of the border image

Computed value:

Same as declared value

Description:

Defines "slice distances," which are offsets from the top, right, bottom, and left edges of the border image. Taken together, they divide the image into nine regions, which correspond to the eight segments of the element's border (four corners and four sides) and the element's background area.

In cases where two opposite regions combine to exceed the total of the dimension they share, both are made completely transparent. For example, if the top slice offset value is 10 and the bottom slice offset value is 20, but the source image is only 25 pixels tall, the two exceed the height of the image. Thus, both the top and bottom segments of the border will be entirely transparent. The same holds for right and left slices and width. Corners are never forcibly made transparent, even in cases where their slices may overlap in the source image.

Examples:

```
div.starry {border-image-slice: 5px;}
aside {border-image-slice: 100 50 150;}
```

Note:

As of early 2011, browsers did not support `border-image-slice`. It is included because `border-image` (which encompasses `border-image-slice`) *was* supported and browsers were expected to add `border-image-slice` support by the end of 2011.

---

border-image-source

Values:

none | <uri>

Initial value:

Applies to:

All elements *except* table elements where `border-collapse` is collapse

Inherited:

No

Percentages:

Refer to the size of the border image

Computed value:

Same as declared value

Description:

Supplies the location of the image to be used as an element's border image.

Examples:

```
div.starry {border-image-source: url(stargrid.png);}
aside {border-image-source: url(asides.png);}
```

Note:

As of early 2011, browsers did not support `border-image-source`. It is included because `border-image` (which encompasses `border-image-source`) *was* supported and browsers were expected to add `border-image-source` support by the end of 2011.

border-image-width

Values:

[<length> | <percentage> | <number> | auto]{1,4}

Initial value:

1

Applies to:

All elements *except* table elements where `border-collapse` is collapse

Inherited:

No

Percentages:

Refer to the size of the border image area

Computed value:

Same as declared value (but see description)

Description:

Defines an image width for each of the four sides of an image border. Border image slices that have a different width than the border image width value are scaled to match it, which may impact how they are repeated. For example, if the right edge of an image border is 10 pixels wide, but `border-image-width: 3px;` has been declared, the border images along the right side are scaled to be three pixels wide.

Note that `border-image-width` is different from `border-width`: a border image's width can be different than the width of the border area. In cases where the image is wider or taller than the border area, it will be clipped by default (but `border-image-outset` may prevent this). If it is narrower or shorter than the border area, it will not be scaled up.

Examples:

```
aside {border-image-width: 8 3 13;}
div#pow{border-image-width: 25px 35;}
```

Note:

As of early 2011, browsers did not support `border-image-width`. It is included because `border-image` (which encompasses `border-image-width`) *was* supported and browsers were expected to add `border-image-width` support by the end of 2011.

border-left

Values:

<'border-width'> || <'border-style'> || <color>

Initial value:

Not defined for shorthand properties

Applies to:

All elements

Inherited:

No

Computed value:

See individual properties

Description:

A shorthand property that property defines the width, color, and style of the left border of an element. As with `border`, omission of a border style will result in no border appearing.

Examples:

```
p {border-left: 3em solid gray;}
pre {border-left: double black 4px;}
```

border-left-color

Values:

<color>

Initial value:

The value of color for the element

Applies to:

All elements

Inherited:

No

Computed value:

If no value is declared, use the computed value of the property color for the same element; otherwise, same as declared value

Description:

Defines the color for the visible portions of the left border of an element. The border's style must be something other than `none` or `hidden` for any visible border to appear.

Examples:

```
p {border-left-color: gray;}
pre {border-left-color: black;}
```

border-left-style

Values:

none | hidden | dotted | dashed | solid | double | groove | ridge | inset | outset

Initial value:

Applies to:

All elements

Inherited:

No

Computed value:

Same as declared value

Description:

Defines the style for the left border of an element. The value must be something other than none for any border to appear.

Examples:

```
p {border-left-style: solid;}
pre {border-left-style: double;}
```

border-left-width

Values:

thin | medium | thick | <length>

Initial value:

medium

Applies to:

All elements

Inherited:

No

Computed value:

Absolute length; 0 if the style of the border is none or hidden

Description:

Defines the width for the left border of an element, which will take effect only if the border's style is something other than none. If the border style is none, the border width is effectively reset to 0. Negative length values are not permitted.

Examples:

```
p {border-left-width: 3em;}
pre {border-left-width: 4px;}
```

border-radius

Values:

[<length> | <percentage>]{1,4} [/ [<length> | <percentage>] {1,4}

Initial value:

0

Applies to:

All elements *except* table elements where border-collapse is collapse

Inherited:

No

Percentages:

Refer to the dimensions of the element's border box (see description)

Computed value:

Same as declared value

Description:

A shorthand property that defines the rounding radius for the bottom-right corner of an element's border. The actual corners will be the height and width declared. For example, suppose the following:

```
.callout {border-radius: 10px;}
```

Each corner of an element with a class of callout will have a rounding that is 10 pixels across, as measured from the beginning of the rounding to the outer side edge of the element, and similarly 10 pixels high. This can be visualized as if the element has 10-pixel-radius (20-pixel-diameter) circles drawn in its corners and the border then bent along the circles' edges.

Note that, given the way the syntax is defined, if two values are supplied, the first applies to the top-left and bottom-right corners, and the second to the top-right and bottom-left corners. To create oval-shaped rounding by supplying one value for the horizontal radius of each corner and a second value for the vertical radii, separate them with a slash:

```
.callout {border-radius: 10px / 20px;}
```

That will cause each of the four corners' rounding to be 10 pixels across and 20 pixels tall. This extends out to setting the four corners uniquely, like so:

```
.callout {border-radius: 10px 20px 30px 40px /
    1em 2em 3em 4em;}
```

This is equivalent to declaring:

```
.callout {border-top-left-radius: 10px 1em;
    border-top-right-radius: 20px 2em;
    border-bottom-right-radius: 30px 3em;
    border-bottom-left-radius: 40px 4em;}
```

Using fewer than four values causes the supplied values to be repeated in the familiar pattern (see margin, padding, etc.) but with a slight offset. Rather than being Top-Right-Bottom-Left (TRBL, or "trouble"), the pattern is TopLeft-TopRight-BottomRight-BottomLeft (TLTRBRBL, or "tilter burble"). Otherwise, the repeat pattern is the same: 1em is the same as 1em 1em 1em 1em, 1em 2em is the same as 1em 2em 1em 2em, and so on. Thus, there can be differing numbers of values to either side of the slash, as the following two declarations are equivalent:

```
.callout {border-radius: 2em 3em 4em / 5%;}
.callout {border-radius: 2em 3em 4em 3em / 5% 5% 5% 5%;}
```

Percentages, when used, are calculated with respect to the size of the element's border box (the box defined by the outer edges of the element's border area) dimension on the related axis. Thus, in the previous declarations, the 5% values are calculated to be 5% of the height of the element's border box because values after the slash define vertical radii. Any percentages used before the slash are calculated as percentages of the width of the element's border box.

Examples:

```
a[href] {border-radius: 0.5em 50%;}
.callout {
    border-radius: 10px 20px 30px 40px /
    1em 2em 3em 4em;}
```

border-right

Values:

<'border-width'> || <'border-style'> || <color>

Initial value:

See individual properties

Applies to:

All elements

Inherited:

No

Computed value:

See individual properties

Description:

A shorthand property that defines the width, color, and style of the right border of an element. As with border, omission of a border style will result in no border appearing.

Examples:

```
img {border-right: 30px dotted blue;}
h3 {border-right: cyan 1em inset;}
```

border-right-color

Values:

<color>

Initial value:

The value of color for the element

Applies to:

All elements

Inherited:

No

Computed value:

If no value is declared, use the computed value of the property color for the same element; otherwise, same as declared value

Description:

Defines the color for the visible portions of the right border of an element. The border's style must be something other than none or hidden for any visible border to appear.

Examples:

```
img {border-right-color: blue;}
h3 {border-right-color: cyan;}
```

border-right-style

Values:

none | hidden | dotted | dashed | solid | double | groove | ridge | inset | outset

Initial value:

Applies to:

All elements

Inherited:

No

Computed value:

Same as declared value

Description:

Defines the style for the right border of an element. The value must be something other than none for any border to appear.

Examples:

```
img {border-right-style: dotted;}
h3 {border-right-style: inset;}
```

border-right-width

Values:

thin | medium | thick | <length>

Initial value:

medium

Applies to:

All elements

Inherited:

No

Computed value:

Absolute length; 0 if the style of the border is none or hidden

Description:

Defines the width for the right border of an element, which will take effect only if the border's style is something other than none. If the border style is none, the border width is effectively reset to 0. Negative length values are not permitted.

Examples:

```
img {border-right-width: 30px;}
h3 {border-right-width: 1em;}
```

border-spacing

Values:

<length> <length>?

Initial value:

0

Applies to:

Elements with a display value of table or inline-table

Inherited:

Yes

Computed value:

Two absolute lengths

Description:

Defines the distance between table cell borders in the separated borders table layout model. The first of the two length values is the horizontal separation and the second is the vertical. This property is only honored when border-collapse is set to separate; otherwise, it is ignored. Although the property applies only to tables, it is inherited by all of the elements within the table.

Examples:

```
table {border-collapse: separate; border-spacing: 0;}
table {border-collapse: separate;
       border-spacing: 3px 5px;}
```

border-style

Values:

[none | hidden | dotted | dashed | solid | double | groove | ridge | inset | outset]{1,4}

Initial value:

Not defined for shorthand properties

Applies to:

All elements

Inherited:

No

Computed value:

See individual properties

Description:

A shorthand property used to define the styles for the overall border of an element or for each side individually. The value of any border must be something other than none for the border to appear. Note that setting border-style to none (its default value) will result in no border at all. In such a case, any value of border-width will be ignored and the width of the border will be set to 0. Any unrecognized value from the list of values should be reinterpreted as solid.

Examples:

```
h1 {border-style: solid;}
img {border-style: inset;}
```

border-top

Values:

<'border-width'> || <'border-style'> || <color>

Initial value:

See individual properties

Applies to:

All elements

Inherited:

No

Computed value:

See individual properties

Description:

A shorthand property that defines the width, color, and style of the top border of an element. As with `border`, omission of a border style will result in no border appearing.

Examples:

```
ul {border-top: 0.5in solid black;}
h1 {border-top: dashed 1px gray;}
```

border-top-color

Values:

<color>

Initial value:

The value of `color` for the element

Applies to:

All elements

Inherited:

No

Computed value:

If no value is declared, use the computed value of the property color for the same element; otherwise, same as declared value

Description:

Sets the color for the visible portions of the top border of an element. The border's style must be something other than none or hidden for any visible border to appear.

Examples:

```
ul {border-top-color: black;}
h1 {border-top-color: gray;}
```

border-top-left-radius

Values:

[<length> | <percentage>] [<length> | <percentage>]?

Initial value:

0

Applies to:

All elements

Inherited:

No

Percentages:

Refer to the dimensions of the element's border box

Computed value:

Same as declared value

Description:

Defines the rounding radius for the top-left corner of an element's border. If two values are supplied, the first is the horizontal radius and the second is the vertical radius. See `border-radius` for a description of how the values create the rounding shape.

Examples:

```
h1 {border-top-left-radius: 10%;}
h2 {border-top-left-radius: 1em 10px;}
```

border-top-right-radius

Values:

[<length> | <percentage>] [<length> | <percentage>]?

Initial value:

0

Applies to:

All elements

Inherited:

No

Percentages:

Refer to the dimensions of the element's border box

Computed value:

Same as declared value

Description:

Defines the rounding radius for the top-right corner of an element's border. If two values are supplied, the first is the horizontal radius and the second is the vertical radius. See `border-radius` for a description of how the values create the rounding shape.

Examples:

```
h1 {border-top-right-radius: 10%;}
h2 {border-top-right-radius: 1em 10px;}
```

border-top-style

Values:

none | hidden | dotted | dashed | solid | double | groove | ridge | inset | outset

Initial value:

Applies to:

All elements

Inherited:

No

Computed value:

Same as declared value

Description:

Defines the style for the top border of an element. The value must be something other than none for any border to appear.

Examples:

```
ul {border-top-style: solid;}
h1 {border-top-style: dashed;}
```

border-top-width

Values:

thin | medium | thick | <length>

Initial value:

Applies to:

All elements

Inherited:

No

Computed value:

Absolute length; 0 if the style of the border is none or hidden

Description:

Defines the width for the top border of an element, which will take effect only if the border's style is something other than none. If the style is none, the width is effectively reset to 0. Negative length values are not permitted.

Examples:

```
ul {border-top-width: 0.5in;}
h1 {border-top-width: 1px;}
```

border-width

Values:

[thin | medium | thick | <length>]{1,4}

Initial value:

Not defined for shorthand properties

Applies to:

All elements

Inherited:

No

Computed value:

See individual properties

Description:

A shorthand property that defines the width for the overall border of an element or for each side individually. The width will take effect for a given border only if the border's style is something other than none. If the border style is none, the border width is effectively reset to 0. Negative length values are not permitted.

Examples:

```
h1 {border-width: 2ex;}
img {border-width: 5px thick thin 1em;}
```

---

bottom

Values:

<length> | <percentage> | auto

Initial value:

auto

Applies to:

Positioned elements (that is, elements for which the value of position is something other than static)

Inherited:

No

Percentages:

Refer to the height of the containing block

Computed value:

For relatively positioned elements, see description; for static elements, auto; for length values, the corresponding absolute length; for percentage values, the declared value; otherwise, auto

Description:

Defines the offset between the bottom outer margin edge of a positioned element and the bottom edge of its containing block. For relatively positioned elements, if both bottom and top are auto, their computed values are both 0; if one of them is auto, it becomes the negative of the other; if neither is auto, bottom will become the negative of the value of top.

Examples:

```
div#footer {position: fixed; bottom: 0;}
sup {position: relative; bottom: 0.5em;
    vertical-align: baseline;}
```

box-align

Values:

stretch | start | end | center | baseline

Initial value:

stretch

Applies to:

Elements with a display value of box or inline-box

Inherited:

No

Computed value:

As declared

Description:

Defines how flexible boxes are laid out along the axis perpendicular to the axis of orientation (see box-orient). The default, stretch, means that the children of the box are stretched to its height (if its box-orient is horizontal) or its width (if its box-orient is vertical). start and end refer to the top and bottom edges of horizontal boxes, and most likely the left and right edges of vertical boxes in left-to-right languages (though this is not specified). center aligns the center of the flexible boxes with the centerline of the axis of orientation.

Examples:

```
div#layout {box-align: stretch;}
.icicle {box-align: start;}
```

Note:

This property is from the 2009 version of the Flexible Box specification. It is expected to be deprecated by a new version of the specification, and potentially retired from browsers some time after.

box-decoration-break

Values:

slice | clone

Initial value:

clone

Applies to:

All elements

Inherited:

No

Computed value:

Same as declared value

Description:

Defines whether the decorations—the background, padding, borders, rounded corners, border image, and box shadow—of a box that has been rendered in multiple pieces are applied to each piece separately or applied to the entire box before it is broken apart.

The most common case is an inline element that wraps across one or more line breaks. With the default behavior, slice, the pieces of the inline element are drawn as though the whole element was laid out in a single line and then sliced apart at each line break. If clone is declared, then each piece of the element is decorated as though they were separate elements sharing the same styles.

box-decoration-break also applies to block boxes that are split across columns or pages.

Examples:

```
span {box-decoration-break: clone;}
a {box-decoration-break: slice;}
```

box-direction

Values:

normal | reverse

Initial value:

normal

Applies to:

Elements with a display value of box or inline-box

Inherited:

No

Computed value:

As declared

Description:

Defines the direction in which the children of a box are laid out. If the value is reverse, then the children are laid out from right to left in a horizontal box, and from bottom to top in a vertical box.

Examples:

```
#tower {box-direction: reverse;}
```

Note:

This property is from the 2009 version of the Flexible Box specification. It is expected to be deprecated by a new version of the specification, and potentially retired from browsers some time after.

box-flex

Values:

<number>

Initial value:

0

Applies to:

Normal-flow children of an element with a `display` value of `box` or `inline-box`

Inherited:

No

Computed value:

As declared

Description:

Defines the "flexibility" of an element that is the child of a box. The `box-flex` values for all the flexible boxes in a group are added together, and then each is divided by that total to get the flexibility. Thus, for example, if three flexible boxes in a group all have a value of `1`, then each has a flexibility of 0.33. If one of them has its `box-flex` value changed to `2`, then it would have a flexibility of 0.5 and the other two would each have a flexibility of 0.25. The default value of 0 indicates that the box is inflexible.

After the flexible boxes are laid out as normal, any extra space left over within the parent box is distributed to the flexible boxes according to its flexibility. To continue the previous example, if there are 100 pixels of space left over, then the `flex-box: 2` element gets 50 pixels added to it, and the other two each get 25 pixels. Similarly, if the flexible boxes overflow the parent box, they are reduced in size proportionately.

Examples:

    #nav li {box-flex: 1;}

Note:

This property is from the 2009 version of the Flexible Box specification. It is expected to be deprecated by a new version of the specification, and potentially retired from browsers some time after.

box-lines

Values:

single | multiple

Initial value:

single

Applies to:

Elements with a `display` value of box or inline-box

Inherited:

No

Computed value:

As declared

Description:

Defines how flexible boxes are laid out if they are too wide to fix in a horizontal box (see `box-orient`). Given the value `multiple`, they will be laid out in as many "lines" as necessary to display them all. This is reminiscent of float layout when multiple floats cannot fit next to one another, though the mechanism is not exactly the same.

Examples:

```
div#gallery {box-lines: multiple;}
```

Note:

This property is from the 2009 version of the Flexible Box specification. It is expected to be deprecated by a new version of the specification, and potentially retired from browsers some time after.

box-ordinal-group

Values:

<integer>

Initial value:

1

Applies to:

Normal-flow children of an element with a display value of box or inline-box

Inherited:

No

Computed value:

As declared

Description:

Defines the ordinal group to which flexible boxes belong. Authors can assign flexible boxes to arbitrary group numbers. When laying out the boxes, the groups are laid out in numeric order, with the flexible boxes within each group arranged according to their source order and the value of box-direction. This allows authors to arrange flexible boxes within their parent box in a manner completely independent of their source order.

Examples:

```
.sticky {box-ordinal-group: 1;}
.footer {box-ordinal-group: 13;}
```

Note:

This property is from the 2009 version of the Flexible Box specification. It is expected to be deprecated by a new version of the specification, and potentially retired from browsers some time after.

box-orient

Values:

horizontal | vertical | inline-axis | block-axis

Initial value:

inline-axis

Applies to:

Elements with a display value of box or inline-box

Inherited:

No

Computed value:

As declared

Description:

Defines the direction in which flexible boxes are arranged within their parent box. horizontal boxes arrange the flexible boxes from left to right, and vertical boxes from top to bottom. inline-axis and block-axis have language-dependent effects; in a left-to-right, top-to-bottom language such as English, they are equivalent to horizontal and vertical.

Examples:

```
#nav {box-orient: horizontal;}
#sidebar {box-orient: vertical;}
```

Note:

This property is from the 2009 version of the Flexible Box specification. It is expected to be deprecated by a new version of the specification, and potentially retired from browsers some time after.

box-pack

Values:

start | end | center | justify

Initial value:

start

Applies to:

Elements with a `display` value of box or inline-box

Inherited:

No

Computed value:

As declared

Description:

Defines how flexible boxes are laid out when the sum of their dimensions along the axis of orientation (see `box-orient`) is less than the total amount of space available.

Examples:

```
#gallery {box-pack: center;}
.subcolumns {box-pack: left;}
```

Note:

This property is from the 2009 version of the Flexible Box specification. It is expected to be deprecated by a new version of the specification, and potentially retired from browsers some time after.

box-shadow

Values:

none | <shadow> [, <shadow>]*

Expansions:

<shadow>

inset? && [<length>{2,4} && <color>?]

Initial value:

Applies to:

All elements

Inherited:

No

Computed value:

As declared with lengths made absolute and colors computed

Description:

Defines one or more shadows that are derived from the shape of the element box. Either outset ("drop") shadows or inset shadows can be defined, the latter with use of the optional inset keyword. Without that keyword, the shadow will be outset.

The four length values that can be declared are, in order: horizontal offset, vertical offset, blur distance, and spread distance. When positive, the offset values go down and the right; when negative, back and to the left. Positive spread values increase the size of the shadow and negative values contract it. Blur values cannot be negative.

Note that all shadows are clipped by the element's border edge. Thus, an outset shadow is only drawn outside the border edge. A semitransparent or fully transparent element background will *not* reveal an outset shadow "behind" the element. Similarly, inset shadows are only visible inside the border edge and are never drawn beyond it.

Examples:

```
h1 {box-shadow: 5px 10px gray;}
table th {
    box-shadow: inset 0.5em 0.75em 5px -2px
    rgba(255,0,0,0.5);}
```

box-sizing

Values:

content-box | border-box

Initial value:

content-box

Applies to:

All elements that accept the width or height properties

Inherited:

No

Computed value:

Same as declared value

Description:

Defines whether the height and width of the element define the dimensions of the content box (the historical behavior) or the border box. If the latter, the value of width defines the distance from the left outer border edge to the right outer border edge; similarly, height defines the distance from the top outer border edge to the bottom outer border edge. Any padding or border widths are "subtracted" from those dimensions instead of the historical "additive" behavior. Thus, given:

```
body {box-sizing: border-box; width: 880px;
    padding: 0 20px;}
```

...the final width of the content area will be 840 pixels (880-20-20).

Examples:

```
body {box-sizing: border-box;}
```

caption-side

Values:

top | bottom

Initial value:

top

Applies to:

Elements with a display of table-caption

Inherited:

Yes

Computed value:

Same as declared value

Description:

Defines the placement of a table caption with respect to the table box. The caption is rendered as though it were a block-level element placed just before (or after) the table.

Examples:

```
caption {caption-side: top;}
```

Note:

The values left and right appeared in CSS2 but were dropped from CSS2.1 because of a lack of widespread support. Some versions of Firefox support left and right.

---

clear

Values:

left | right | both | none

Initial value:

Applies to:

Block-level elements

Inherited:

No

Computed value:

Same as declared value

Description:

Defines to which side (or sides) of an element no floating element may be placed. If normal layout of a cleared element would result in a floated element appearing on the cleared side, the cleared element is pushed down until it sits below (clears) the floated element. In CSS1 and CSS2, this is accomplished by automatically increasing the top margin of the cleared element. In CSS2.1, clearance space is added above the element's top margin, but the margin itself is not altered. In either case, the end result is that the element's top outer border edge is just below the bottom outer margin edge of a floated element on the declared side.

Examples:

```
h1 {clear: both;}
p + h3 {clear: right;}
```

clip

Values:

rect(*top, right, bottom, left*) | auto

Initial value:

auto

Applies to:

Absolutely positioned elements (in CSS2, clip applied to block-level and replaced elements)

Inherited:

No

Computed value:

For a rectangle, a set of four computed lengths representing the edges of the clipping rectangle; otherwise, same as declared value

Description:

Defines a clipping rectangle inside of which the content of an absolutely positioned element is visible. Content outside the clipping area is treated according to the value of overflow. The clipping area can be smaller or larger than the content area of the element, the latter being accomplished with negative length values.

In current browsers, the clipping area is defined by using the rect() value to define the offsets of the top, right, bottom, and left edges of the clipping areas with respect to the top-left corner of the element. Thus, the value rect(5px, 10px, 40px, 5px) would place the top edge of the clipping area 5px down from the top edge of the element, the right edge of the clipping area 10 pixels to the right of the left edge of the element, the bottom edge of the clipping area 40 pixels down from the top edge of the element, and the left edge of the clipping area 5 pixels to the right of the left edge of the element.

Examples:

```
div.sidebar {overflow: scroll; clip: 0 0 5em 10em;}
img.tiny {overflow: hidden; clip: 5px 5px 20px 20px;}
```

---

color

Values:

<color>

Initial value:

User agent–specific

Applies to:

All elements

Inherited:

Yes

Computed value:

See description

Description:

Defines the foreground color of an element, which in HTML rendering means the text of an element; raster images are not affected by color. This is also the color applied to any borders of the element, unless overridden by border-color or one of the other border color properties (border-top-color, etc.).

In the case of color keywords (such as navy) and RGB hex values (such as #008800 or #080), the computed value is the rgb() equivalent. For transparent, the computed value is rgba(0,0,0,0); for currentColor, the computed value is inherit. For all other values, the computed value is the same as the declared value.

Examples:

```
strong {color: rgb(255,128,128);}
h3 {color: navy;}
p.warning {color: #ff0000;}
pre.pastoral {color: rgba(0%,100%,0%,0.33334);}
```

column-count

Values:

<integer> | auto

Initial value:

auto

Applies to:

Nonreplaced block-level elements (except table elements), table cells, and inline-block elements

Inherited:

No

Computed value:

Same as declared value

Description:

Defines the number of columns used in a multicolumn layout of an element. Besides the default auto, only positive nonzero integers are permitted.

Examples:

```
body {column-count: 2;}
```

column-fill

Values:

auto | balance

Initial value:

balance

Applies to:

Elements laid out using multiple columns

Inherited:

No

Computed value:

Same as declared value

Description:

Defines how the columns in an element laid out with multiple columns are height-balanced (or not). This property's value only takes hold in cases where the column lengths have been in some way constrained. The obvious case of this would be if the element's height has been explicitly set. In all other cases, the columns are automatically balanced. The value auto means columns are filled sequentially, which is to say each column is filled to the full column height until the last, which is either under- or over-filled as necessary.

Examples:

```
body {height: 50em; column-fill: auto;}
```

column-gap

Values:
<length> | normal

Initial value:
normal

Applies to:
Elements laid out using multiple columns

Inherited:
No

Computed value:
Same as declared value

Description:
Defines the width of the gap between adjacent columns in an element laid out with multiple columns. Any column rule (see column-rule) is centered within each gap. Gap lengths cannot be negative.

Examples:
```
body {column-gap: 2em;}
```

column-rule

Values:
<'column-rule-width'> || <'border-style'> || [<color>

Initial value:
See individual properties

Applies to:
Elements laid out using multiple columns

Inherited:

No

Computed value:

Same as declared value

Description:

A shorthand property that defines the width, style, and color of the "rules" (vertical lines) drawn between columns in an element laid out with multiple columns. Any value omitted is set to the default value of the corresponding property. Note that if no border style is defined, it will default to none and no column rule will be drawn.

Examples:

```
#d01 {column-rule: 5px solid red;}
#d02 {column-rule: 2em dashed green;}
```

column-rule-color

Values:

<color>

Initial value:

User agent–specific

Applies to:

Elements laid out using multiple columns

Inherited:

No

Computed value:

Same as declared value

Description:

Defines the color of the "rules" (vertical lines) drawn between columns in an element laid out with multiple columns.

Examples:

```
#d01 {column-rule-color: red;}
#d02 {column-rule-color: green;}
```

column-rule-style

Values:

<'border-style'>

Initial value:

Applies to:

Elements laid out using multiple columns

Inherited:

No

Computed value:

Same as declared value

Description:

Defines the style of the "rules" (vertical lines) drawn between columns in an element laid out with multiple columns. The values are the same as for the property `border-style`. Either of the values none (the default) or hidden means no rule will be drawn.

Examples:

```
#d01 {column-rule-style: solid;}
#d02 {column-rule-style: dashed;}
```

column-rule-width

Values:

thin | medium | thick | <length>

Initial value:

medium

Applies to:

Elements laid out using multiple columns

Inherited:

No

Computed value:

Absolute length; 0 if the style of the border is none or hidden

Description:

Defines the width of the "rules" (vertical lines) drawn between columns in an element laid out with multiple columns.

Examples:

```
#d01 {column-rule-width: 5px;}
#d02 {column-rule-width: 2em;}
```

column-span

Values:

none | all

Initial value:

Applies to:

Static-position nonfloating elements

Inherited:

No

Computed value:

Same as declared value

Description:

Defines the number of columns an element spans in an element laid out with multiple columns. There are only two options: to span no columns at all (none) or to span all columns (all). When an element spans multiple columns, content that comes before it is balanced above it across the columns. Content that comes after is balanced below the spanning element.

Examples:

```
h2 {column-span: all;}
```

column-width

Values:

<length> | auto

Initial value:

auto

Applies to:

Nonreplaced block-level elements (except table elements), table cells, and inline-block elements

Inherited:

No

Computed value:

Absolute length

Description:

Defines the optimal widths of the columns in an element laid out with multiple columns. Note that this describes an *optimal* width, and as such, user agents may modify or ignore the value if they see fit. The obvious example is if the sum total of the width of the columns and their gaps does not equal the width of the multicolumn element. In such cases, the column widths will be altered to make the columns fit the element. This is somewhat similar in nature to altering the width of table cells so that the table columns fit the table's total width.

Length values must be greater than zero. For some reason, percentages are not permitted.

Examples:

```
body {column-width: 23em;}
```

columns

Values:

<'column-width'> || <'column-count'>

Initial value:

See individual properties

Applies to:

Nonreplaced block-level elements (except table elements), table cells, and inline-block elements

Inherited:

No

Computed value:

Same as declared value

Description:

A shorthand property used to define the number and width of the columns in an element laid out with multiple columns. Omitted values are set to the default values for the corresponding properties.

Examples:

```
body {columns: 3 23em;}
div {columns: 200px 5;}
```

content

Values:

normal | none | [<string> | <uri> | <counter> | attr(<identifier>) | open-quote | close-quote | no-open-quote | no-close-quote]+

Initial value:

normal

Applies to:

::before and ::after pseudo-elements

Inherited:

No

Computed value:

For <uri> values, an absolute URI; for attribute references, the resulting string; otherwise, same as declared value

Description:

Defines the generated content placed before or after an element. By default, this is likely to be inline content, but the type of box the content creates can be defined using the property display.

Examples:

```
p::before {content: "Paragraph...";}
a[href]::after {content: "(" attr(href) ")";
     font-size: smaller;}
```

counter-increment

Values:

[<identifier> <integer>?]+ | none

Initial value:

Applies to:

All elements

Inherited:

No

Computed value:

Same as declared value

Description:

With this property, counters can be incremented (or decremented) by any value, positive or negative or 0. If no <integer> is supplied, it defaults to 1.

Examples:

```
h1 {counter-increment: section;}
*.backward li {counter-increment: counter -1;}
```

counter-reset

Values:

[<identifier> <integer>?]+ | none

Initial value:

Applies to:

All elements

Inherited:

No

Computed value:

Same as declared value

Description:

With this property, counters can be reset (or set for the first time) to any value, positive or negative. If no <integer> is supplied, it defaults to 0.

Examples:

```
h1 {counter-reset: section;}
h2 {counter-reset: subsec 1;}
```

---

cursor

Values:

[<uri> [<number> <number>]?,]* [auto | default | auto | default | none | context-menu | help | pointer | progress | wait | cell | cross hair | text | vertical-text | alias | copy | move | no-drop | not-allowed | e-resize | n-resize | ne-resize | nw-resize | s-resize | se-resize | sw-resize | w-resize | ew-resize | ns-resize | nesw-resize | nwse-resize | col-resize | row-resize | all-scroll]

Initial value:

auto

Applies to:

All elements

Inherited:

Yes

Computed value:

For <uri> values, given that a <uri> resolves to a supported file type, a single absolute URI with optional X,Y coordinates; otherwise, same as declared keyword

Description:

Defines the cursor shape to be used when a mouse pointer is placed within the boundary of an element (although CSS2.1 does not define which edge creates the boundary). Authors are cautioned to remember that users are typically very aware of cursor changes and can be easily confused by changes that seem counterintuitive. For example, making any noninteractive element switch the cursor state to `pointer` is quite likely to cause user frustration.

Note that the value syntax makes URI values optional, but the keyword mandatory. Thus you can specify any number of URIs to external cursor resources, but the value *must* end with a keyword. Leaving off the keyword will cause conforming user agents to drop the declaration entirely.

CSS3 allows two numbers to be supplied with a <uri> value. These define the X,Y coordinates of the cursor's "active point"; that is, the point in the cursor that is used for determining hover states, active actions, and so forth. If no numbers are supplied and the cursor image has no "intrinsic hotspot" (to quote the specification), the top-left corner of the image is used (equivalent to `0 0`). Note that the numbers are unitless and are interpreted relative to the "cursor's coordinate system" (to quote again).

Examples:

```
a.moreinfo {cursor: help;}
a[href].external {cursor: url(globe.png), auto;}
```

---

direction

Values:

ltr | rtl

Initial value:

ltr

Applies to:

All elements

Inherited:

Yes

Computed value:

Same as declared value

Description:

Defines the base writing direction of blocks and the direction of embeddings and overrides for the unicode bidirectional algorithm. Furthermore, it changes the way a number of properties and layout decisions are handled, including but not limited to the placement of table cells in a table row and the layout algorithms for block boxes.

For a variety of reasons, authors are strongly encouraged to use the HTML attribute dir rather than the CSS property direction. User agents that do not support bidirectional text are permitted to ignore this property.

Examples:

```
*:lang(en) {direction: ltr;}
*:lang(ar) {direction: rtl;}
```

display

CSS2.1 values:

none | inline | block | inline-block | list-item | table | inline-table | table-row-group | table-header-group | table-footer-group | table-row | table-column-group | table-column | table-cell | table-caption

CSS3 values:

none | inline | block | inline-block | list-item | run-in | compact | table | inline-table | table-row-group | table-header-group | table-footer-group | table-row | table-column-group | table-column | table-cell | table-caption | ruby | ruby-base | ruby-text | ruby-base-container | ruby-text-container

Initial value:

inline

Applies to:

All elements

Inherited:

No

Computed value:

Varies for floated, positioned, and root elements (see CSS2.1, section 9.7); otherwise, same as declared value

Description:

Defines the kind of display box an element generates during layout. Gratuitous use of display with a document type such as HTML can be tricky, as it upsets the display hierarchy already defined in HTML, but it can also be very useful. In the case of XML, which has no such built-in hierarchy, display is indispensable.

The value none is often used to make elements "disappear," since it removes the element and all of its descendant elements from the presentation. This is true not just in visual media, but in all media; thus, setting an element to display: none will prevent it from being spoken by a speaking browser.

The value run-in was long a part of CSS2.1 but was dropped in early 2011 because of inconsistencies among browsers. It is still listed as part of CSS3. The values compact and marker appeared in CSS2 but were dropped from CSS2.1 because of a lack of widespread support.

Examples:

```
h1 {display: block;}
li {display: list-item;}
img {display: inline;}
.hide {display: none;}
tr {display: table-row;}
```

empty-cells

Values:

show | hide

Initial value:

show

Applies to:

Elements with a `display` value of `table-cell`

Inherited:

Yes

Computed value:

Same as declared value

Description:

Defines the presentation of table cells that contain no content. If shown, the cell's borders and background are drawn. This property is only honored if `border-collapse` is set to `separate`; otherwise, it is ignored.

Examples:

```
th, td {empty-cells: show;}
```

---

float

Values:

`left` | `right` | `none`

Initial value:

Applies to:

All elements

Inherited:

No

Computed value:

Same as declared value

Description:

Defines the direction in which an element is floated. This has traditionally been applied to images in order to let text flow around

them, but in CSS, any element may be floated. A floated element
will generate a block-level box no matter what kind of element it
may be. Floated nonreplaced elements should be given an explicit
width, as they otherwise tend to become as narrow as possible.
Floating is generally well supported by all browsers, but the nature
of floats can lead to unexpected results when they are used as a page
layout mechanism. This is largely due to subtle differences in the
interpretation of statements like "as narrow as possible."

Examples:

```
img.figure {float: left;}
p.sidebar {float: right; width: 15em;}
```

---

font

Values:

[[<'font-style'> || <'font-variant'> || <'font-weight'>]? <'font-
size'> [/ <'line-height'>]? <'font-family'>] | caption | icon | menu |
message-box | small-caption | status-bar

Initial value:

Refer to individual properties

Applies to:

All elements

Inherited:

Yes

Percentages:

Calculated with respect to the parent element for <font-size> and
with respect to the element's <font-size> for <line-height>

Computed value:

See individual properties

Description:

A shorthand property used to set all the aspects of an element's font
at once. It can also be used to set the element's font to match an
aspect of the user's computing environment using keywords such
as icon. If keywords are not used, the minimum font value *must*
include the font size and family *in that order*, and any font value
that is not a keyword must end with the font family. Otherwise, the
font declaration will be ignored.

Examples:

```
p {font: small-caps italic bold small/
    1.25em Helvetica,sans-serif;}
p.example {font: 14px Arial;} /* technically correct,
    although generic font-families are encouraged for
    fallback purposes */
.figure span {font: icon;}
```

---

font-family

Values:

[<family-name> | <generic-family>] [, <family-name>| <generic-family>]*

Expansions:

<generic-family>

serif | sans-serif | monospace | cursive | fantasy

Initial value:

User agent–specific

Applies to:

All elements

Inherited:

Yes

Computed value:

Same as declared value

Description:

Defines a font family to be used in the display of an element's text. Note that use of a specific font family (e.g., Geneva) is wholly dependent on that family being available, either on the user's computer or thanks to a downloadable font file, and the font family containing the glyphs needed to display the content. Therefore, using generic family names as a fallback is strongly encouraged. Font names that contain spaces or nonalphabetic characters should be quoted to minimize potential confusion. In contrast, generic fallback family names should *never* be quoted.

Examples:

```
p {font-family: Helvetica, Arial, sans-serif;}
li {font-family: Times, TimesNR, "New Century Schoolbook",
serif;}
pre {font-family: Courier, "Courier New", "Andale Mono",
Monaco, monospace;}
```

font-size

Values:

xx-small | x-small | small | medium | large | x-large | xx-large | smaller | larger | <length> | <percentage>

Initial value:

medium

Applies to:

All elements

Inherited:

Yes

Percentages:

Calculated with respect to the parent element's font size

Computed value:

An absolute length

Description:

Defines the size of the font. The size can be defined as an absolute size, a relative size, a length value, or a percentage value. Negative length and percentage values are not permitted. The dangers of font-size assignment are many and varied, and points are particularly discouraged in web design, as there is no certain relationship between points and the pixels on a monitor. It's a matter of historical interest that because of early misunderstandings, setting the `font-size` to `medium` led to different results in early versions of Internet Explorer and Navigator 4.x. Some of these problems are covered in Chapter 5 of *CSS: The Definitive Guide*, third edition (O'Reilly); for further discussion, refer to *http://style.cleverchimp .com/*. For best results, authors are encouraged to use either percentages or em units for font sizing. As a last resort, pixel sizes can be used, but this approach has serious accessibility penalties because it prevents users from resizing text in IE/Win, even when it is too small to read comfortably. Most other browsers allow users to resize text regardless of how it has been sized.

Examples:

```
h2 {font-size: 200%;}
code {font-size: 0.9em;}
p.caption {font-size: 9px;}
```

---

font-size-adjust

Values:

<number> | none

Initial value:

Applies to:

All elements

Inherited:

Yes

Computed value:

Same as declared value

Description:

Defines an *aspect value* for the element, which is used to scale fonts such that they more closely match each other in cases where fallback fonts are used. The proper aspect value for a font is its true x-height divided by its font size.

How `font-size-adjust` actually works is to size fonts according to their x-height, which is to say according to the height of lowercase letters. For example, consider a hypothetical font (let's call it "CSSType") that, when set to a font size of 100 pixels, has an x-height of 60 pixels; that is, its lowercase "x" letterform is 60 pixels tall. The appropriate `font-size-adjust` value for CSSType is thus 0.6. Declaring:

```
p {font: 20px "CSSType", sans-serif;
    font-size-adjust: 0.6;}
```

...means that paragraph text should be sized so that lowercase letters are 12 pixels tall (20 × 0.6 = 12), *no matter what font family is used*. If CSSType is unavailable and the user agent falls back to (for example) Helvetica, the Helvetica text will be sized so that lowercase letters are 12 pixels tall and the uppercase letters will be whatever size results. Since the aspect value of Helvetica is 0.53, its uppercase letters will be 22.6 pixels tall (or a rounded-off value, if the user agent can't handle fractional pixels). If some other sans-serif font is used and its aspect value is 0.7, the uppercase letters of that text will be 17.1 pixels tall while its lowercase letters will still be 12 pixels tall.

Examples:

```
body {font-family: Helvetica, sans-serif;
    font-size-adjust: 0.53;}
```

---

font-style

Values:

italic | oblique | normal

Initial value:

normal

Applies to:

All elements

Inherited:

Yes

Computed value:

Same as declared value

Description:

Defines whether the font uses an italic, oblique, or normal font face. Italic text is generally defined as a separate face within the font family. It is theoretically possible for a user agent to compute a slanted font face from the normal face. In reality, user agents rarely (if at all) recognize the difference between italic and oblique text and almost always render both in exactly the same way.

Examples:

```
em {font-style: oblique;}
i {font-style: italic;}
```

font-variant

Values:

small-caps | normal

Initial value:

normal

Applies to:

All elements

Inherited:

Yes

Computed value:

Same as declared value

Description:

Defines whether text is set in the small-caps style. It is theoretically possible for a user agent to compute a small-caps font face from the normal face.

Examples:

```
h3 {font-variant: small-caps;}
p {font-variant: normal;}
```

font-weight

Values:

normal | bold | bolder | lighter | 100 | 200 | 300 | 400 | 500 | 600 | 700 | 800 | 900

Initial value:

normal

Applies to:

All elements

Inherited:

Yes

Computed value:

One of the numeric values (100, etc.) or one of the numeric values plus one of the relative values (bolder or lighter)

Description:

Defines font weight used in rendering an element's text. The numeric value 400 is equivalent to the keyword normal, and 700 is equivalent to bold. If a font has only two weights—normal and bold—the numbers 100 through 500 will be normal, and 600 through 900 will be bold. In general terms, the visual result of each

numeric value must be at least as light as the next lowest number
and at least as heavy as the next highest number.

Examples:

```
b {font-weight: 700;}
strong {font-weight: bold;}
.delicate {font-weight: lighter;}
```

height

Values:

<length> | <percentage> | auto

Initial value:

auto

Applies to:

All elements *except* nonreplaced inline elements, table columns,
and column groups

Inherited:

No

Percentages:

Calculated with respect to the height of the containing block

Computed value:

For auto and percentage values, as declared; otherwise, an absolute
length, unless the property does not apply to the element (then auto)

Description:

Defines the height of either an element's content area or its border
box, depending on the value of box-sizing. Negative length and
percentage values are not permitted.

Examples:

```
img.icon {height: 50px;}
h1 {height: 1.75em;}
```

left

Values:

<length> | <percentage> | auto

Initial value:

auto

Applies to:

Positioned elements (that is, elements for which the value of position is something other than static)

Inherited:

No

Percentages:

Refer to the width of the containing block

Computed value:

For relatively positioned elements, left always equals –right; for static elements, auto; for length values, the corresponding absolute length; for percentage values, the declared value; otherwise, auto

Description:

Defines the offset between the left outer margin edge of an absolutely positioned element and the left edge of its containing block; or, for relatively positioned elements, the distance by which the element is offset to the right of its starting position.

Examples:

```
div#footer {position: fixed; left: 0;}
*.hanger {position: relative; left: -25px;}
```

letter-spacing

Values:

[normal | <length> | <percentage>]{1,3}

Initial value:

normal

Applies to:

All elements

Inherited:

Yes

Percentages:

Refer to the width of the Unicode space glyph (U+0020) of the element's font face

Computed value:

For length values, the absolute length; otherwise, normal

Description:

Defines the amount of whitespace to be inserted between the character boxes of text. Because character glyphs are typically narrower than their character boxes, length values create a modifier to the usual spacing between letters. Thus, normal is (most likely) synonymous with 0. Negative length and percentage values are permitted and will cause letters to bunch closer together.

The three possible values correspond to the minimum, maximum, and optimal spacing between letters. If two values are listed, the first corresponds to the minimum and optimal spacing and the second to the maximum spacing. If a single value is listed, it is used for all three. If the text is justified, the user agent may exceed the maximum spacing if necessary, but it is never supposed to go below the minimum spacing. For nonjustified text, the optimal spacing is always used.

Examples:

```
p.spacious {letter-spacing: 6px;}
em {letter-spacing: 0.2em;}
p.cramped {letter-spacing: -0.5em;}
```

Note:

In CSS2.1, letter-spacing only accepts a single value: a length or normal.

line-height

Values:

<length> | <percentage> | <number> | normal | none

Initial value:

normal

Applies to:

All elements (but see text regarding replaced and block-level elements)

Inherited:

Yes

Percentages:

Relative to the font size of the element

Computed value:

For length and percentage values, the absolute value; otherwise, same as declared value

Description:

This property influences the layout of line boxes. When applied to a block-level element, it defines the minimum (but not the maximum) distance between baselines within that element. When applied to an inline element, it is used to define the *leading* of that element.

The difference between the computed values of line-height and font-size (called "leading" in CSS) is split in half and added to the top and bottom of each piece of content in a line of text. The shortest box that can enclose all those pieces of content is the line box.

A raw number value assigns a scaling factor, which is inherited instead of a computed value. Negative values are not permitted.

Examples:

```
p {line-height: 1.5em;}
h2 {line-height: 200%;}
ul {line-height: 1.2;}
pre {line-height: 0.75em;}
```

Note:

The keyword none was added in CSS3 and is not supported as of early 2011.

list-style

Values:

<list-style-type> || <list-style-image> || <list-style-position>

Initial value:

Refer to individual properties

Applies to:

Elements whose display value is list-item

Inherited:

Yes

Computed value:

See individual properties

Description:

A shorthand property that defines the marker type, whether a symbol or an image, and its (crude) placement. Because it applies to any element that has a display of list-item, it will apply only to li elements in ordinary HTML and XHTML, although it can be applied to any element and subsequently inherited by list-item elements.

Examples:

```
ul {list-style: square url(bullet3.gif) outer;}
    /* values are inherited by 'li' elements */
ol {list-style: upper-roman;}
```

list-style-image

Values:

<uri> | none

Initial value:

Applies to:

Elements whose display value is list-item

Inherited:

Yes

Computed value:

For <uri> values, the absolute URI; otherwise, none

Description:

Specifies an image to be used as the marker on an ordered or un-ordered list item. The placement of the image with respect to the content of the list item can be crudely controlled using list-style-position.

Examples:

```
ul {list-style-image: url(bullet3.gif);}
ul li {list-style-image: url(http://example.org/pix/
checkmark.png);}
```

list-style-position

Values:

inside | outside

Initial value:

outside

Applies to:

Elements whose display value is list-item

Inherited:

Yes

Computed value:

Same as declared value

Description:

Defines the position of the list marker with respect to the content of the list item. Outside markers are placed some distance from the border edge of the list item, but the distance is not defined in CSS. Inside markers are treated as though they were inline elements inserted at the beginning of the list item's content.

Examples:

```
li {list-style-position: outside;}
ol li {list-style-position: inside;}
```

list-style-type

CSS2.1 values:

disc | circle | square | decimal | decimal-leading-zero | upper-alpha | lower-alpha | upper-latin | lower-latin | upper-roman | lower-roman | lower-greek | georgian | armenian | none

CSS3 values:

\<glyph> | \<algorithmic> | \<numeric> | \<alphabetic> | \<symbolic> | \<non-repeating> | normal | none

Expansions:

\<glyph>

box | check | circle | diamond | disc | hyphen | square

`<algorithmic>`

armenian | cjk-ideographic | ethiopic-numeric | georgian | hebrew | japanese-formal | japanese-informal | lower-armenian | lower-roman | simp-chinese-formal | simp-chinese-informal | syriac | tamil | trad-chinese-formal | trad-chinese-informal | upper-armenian | upper-roman

`<numeric>`

arabic-indic | binary | bengali | cambodian | decimal | decimal-leading-zero | devanagari | gujarati | gurmukhi | kannada | khmer | lao | lower-hexadecimal | malayalam | mongolian | myanmar | octal | oriya | persian | telugu | tibetan | thai | upper-hexadecimal | urdu

`<alphabetic>`

afar | amharic | amharic-abegede | cjk-earthly-branch | cjk-heavenly-stem | ethiopic | ethiopic-abegede | ethiopic-abegede-am-et | ethiopic-abegede-gez | ethiopic-abegede-ti-er | ethiopic-abegede-ti-et | ethiopic-halehame-aa-er | ethiopic-halehame-aa-et | ethiopic-halehame-am-et | ethiopic-halehame-gez | ethiopic-halehame-om-et | ethiopic-halehame-sid-et | ethiopic-halehame-so-et | ethiopic-halehame-ti-er | ethiopic-halehame-ti-et | ethiopic-halehame-tig | hangul | hangul-consonant | hiragana | hiragana-iroha | katakana | katakana-iroha | lower-alpha | lower-greek | lower-norwegian | lower-latin | oromo | sidama | somali | tigre | tigrinya-er | tigrinya-er-abegede | tigrinya-et | tigrinya-et-abegede | upper-alpha | upper-greek | upper-norwegian | upper-latin

`<symbolic>`

asterisks | footnotes

`<non-repeating>`

circled-decimal | circled-lower-latin | circled-upper-latin | dotted-decimal | double-circled-decimal | filled-circled-decimal | parenthesised-decimal | parenthesised-lower-latin

Initial value:

disc

Applies to:

Elements whose `display` value is `list-item`

Inherited:

Yes

Computed value:

Same as declared value

Description:

Defines the type of marker system to be used in the presentation of a list. CSS3 provides a greatly expanded number of list types, but as of early 2011, support for these newer list types was spotty. Use extra caution when using list types beyond those provided by CSS2.1.

There is no defined behavior for what happens when a list using an alphabetic ordering exceeds the letters in the list. For example, once an `upper-latin` list reaches "Z," the specification does not say what the next bullet should be. (Two possible answers are "AA" and "ZA.") This is the case regardless of the alphabet in use. Thus, there is no guarantee that different user agents will act consistently.

Examples:

```
ul {list-style-type: square;}
ol {list-style-type: lower-roman;}
```

Note:

As of this writing, the only CSS2.1 values with widespread support are `disc`, `circle`, `square`, `decimal`, `upper-alpha`, `lower-alpha`, `upper-latin`, `upper-roman`, and `lower-roman`.

margin

Values:

[<length> | <percentage> | auto]{1,4}

Initial value:

Not defined

Applies to:

All elements

Inherited:

No

Percentages:

Refer to the width of the containing block

Computed value:

See individual properties

Description:

A shorthand property that defines the width of the overall margin for an element or sets distinct widths for the individual side margins. Vertically adjacent margins of block-level elements are collapsed, whereas inline elements effectively do not take top and bottom margins. The left and right margins of inline elements do not collapse, nor do margins on floated elements. Negative margin values are permitted, but caution is warranted because negative values can cause elements to overlap other elements or to appear to be wider than their parent elements.

Examples:

```
h1 {margin: 2ex;}
p {margin: auto;}
img {margin: 10px;}
```

margin-bottom

Values:

<length> | <percentage> | auto

Initial value:

0

Applies to:

All elements

Inherited:

No

Percentages:

Refer to the width of the containing block

Computed value:

For percentages, as declared; for length values, the absolute length

Description:

Defines the width of the bottom margin for an element. Negative values are permitted, but caution is warranted (see margin).

Examples:

```
ul {margin-bottom: 0.5in;}
h1 {margin-bottom: 2%;}
```

margin-left

Values:

<length> | <percentage> | auto

Initial value:

0

Applies to:

All elements

Inherited:

No

Percentages:

Refer to the width of the containing block

Computed value:

For percentages, as declared; for length values, the absolute length

Description:

Defines the width of the left margin for an element. Negative values are permitted, but caution is warranted (see margin).

Examples:

```
p {margin-left: 5%;}
pre {margin-left: 3em;}
```

margin-right

Values:

<length> | <percentage> | auto

Initial value:

0

Applies to:

All elements

Inherited:

No

Percentages:

Refer to the width of the containing block

Computed value:

For percentages, as declared; for length values, the absolute length

Description:

Defines the width of the right margin for an element. Negative values are permitted, but caution is warranted (see margin).

Examples:

```
img {margin-right: 30px;}
ol {margin-right: 5em;}
```

margin-top

Values:

<length> | <percentage> | auto

Initial value:

0

Applies to:

All elements

Inherited:

No

Percentages:

Refer to the width of the containing block

Computed value:

For percentages, as declared; for length values, the absolute length

Description:

Defines the width of the top margin for an element. Negative values are permitted, but caution is warranted (see margin).

Examples:

```
ul {margin-top: 0.5in;}
h3 {margin-top: 1.5em;}
```

max-height

Values:

<length> | <percentage> | none

Initial value:

Applies to:

All elements except inline nonreplaced elements and table elements

Inherited:

No

Percentages:

Refer to the height of the containing block

Computed value:

For percentages, as declared; for length values, the absolute length; otherwise, none

Description:

Defines a maximum constraint on the height of the element (the exact nature of that height is dependent on the value of box-sizing). Thus, the element can be shorter than the declared value but not taller. Negative values are not permitted.

Example:

```
div#footer {max-height: 3em;}
```

max-width

Values:

<length> | <percentage> | none

Initial value:

Applies to:

All elements except inline nonreplaced elements and table elements

Inherited:

No

Percentages:

Refer to the height of the containing block

Computed value:

For percentages, as declared; for length values, the absolute length; otherwise, none

Description:

Defines a maximum constraint on the width of the element (the exact nature of that width is dependent on the value of box-sizing). Thus, the element can be narrower than the declared value but not wider. Negative values are not permitted.

Example:

```
#sidebar img {width: 50px; max-width: 100%;}
```

---

min-height

Values:

<length> | <percentage>

Initial value:

0

Applies to:

All elements except inline nonreplaced elements and table elements

Inherited:

No

Percentages:

Refer to the width of the containing block

Computed value:

For percentages, as declared; for length values, the absolute length

Description:

Defines a minimum constraint on the height of the element (the exact nature of that height is dependent on the value of box-sizing). Thus, the element can be taller than the declared value, but not shorter. Negative values are not permitted.

Example:

```
div#footer {min-height: 1em;}
```

min-width

Values:

<length> | <percentage>

Initial value:

0

Applies to:

All elements except inline nonreplaced elements and table elements

Inherited:

No

Percentages:

Refer to the width of the containing block

Computed value:

For percentages, as declared; for length values, the absolute length; otherwise, none

Description:

Defines a minimum constraint on the width of the element (the exact nature of that width is dependent on the value of box-sizing). Thus, the element can be wider than the declared value, but not narrower. Negative values are not permitted.

Example:

```
div.aside {float: right; width: 13em; max-width: 33%;}
```

opacity

Values:

<number>

Initial value:

1

Applies to:

All elements

Inherited:

No

Computed value:

Same as declared (or a clipped value if declared value must be clipped)

Description:

Defines an element's degree of opacity using a number in the range 0–1, inclusive. Any values outside that range are clipped to the nearest edge (0 or 1). This property affects every visible portion of an element. If it is necessary to have the content of an element semiopaque but not the background, or vice versa, use alpha color types such as rgba().

An element with opacity of 0 is effectively invisible and may not respond to mouse or other DOM events. Because of the way semiopaque elements are expected to be drawn, an element with opacity less than 1.0 creates its own stacking context even if it is not positioned. For similar reasons, an absolutely positioned element with opacity less than 1 and a z-index of auto force-alters the z-index value to 0.

Examples:

```
h2 {opacity: 0.8;}
.hideme {opacity: 0;}
```

outline

Values:

<'outline-color'> || <'outline-style'> || <'outline-width'>

Initial value:

Not defined for shorthand properties

Applies to:

All elements

Inherited:

No

Computed value:

See individual properties

Description:

This is a shorthand property that defines the overall outline for an element. The most common use of outlines is to indicate which form element or hyperlink currently has focus (accepts keyboard input). Outlines can be of irregular shape, and no matter how thick, they do not change or otherwise affect the placement of elements.

Examples:

```
*[href]:focus {outline: 2px dashed invert;}
form:focus {outline: outset cyan 0.25em;}
```

outline-color

Values:

<color> | invert

Initial value:

invert (see description)

Applies to:

All elements

Inherited:

No

Computed value:

Same as declared value

Description:

Defines the color for the visible portions of the overall outline of an element. Remember that the value of outline-style must be something other than none for any visible border to appear. User agents are permitted to ignore invert on platforms that don't support color inversion. In that case, the outline's color defaults to the value of color for the element.

Examples:

```
*[href]:focus {outline-color: invert;}
form:focus {outline-color: cyan;}
```

outline-offset

Values:

Initial value:

0

Applies to:

All elements

Inherited:

No

Computed value:

An absolute length value

Description:

Defines the offset distance between the outer border edge and inner outline edge. Only one length value can be supplied and it applies equally to all sides of the outline. Values can be negative, which causes the outline to "shrink" inward toward the element's center. Note that outline-offset cannot be set via the shorthand outline.

Examples:

```
*[href]:focus {outline-offset: 0.33em;}
form:focus {outline-offset: -1px;}
```

outline-style

Values:

none | dotted | dashed | solid | double | groove | ridge | inset | outset

Initial value:

Applies to:

All elements

Inherited:

No

Computed value:

Same as declared value

Description:

Defines the style for the overall border of an element. The style must be something other than none for any outline to appear.

Examples:

```
*[href]:focus {outline-style: dashed;}
form:focus {outline-style: outset;}
```

outline-width

Values:

thin | medium | thick | <length>

Initial value:

medium

Applies to:

All elements

Inherited:

No

Computed value:

Absolute length; 0 if the style of the border is none or hidden

Description:

Defines the width for the overall outline of an element. The width will take effect only for a given outline if the value of outline-style is something other than none. If the style *is* none, the width is effectively reset to 0. Negative length values are not permitted.

Examples:

```
*[href]:focus {outline-width: 2px;}
form:focus {outline-width: 0.25em;}
```

overflow

Values:

[visible | hidden | scroll | auto | no-display | no-content]{1,2}

Initial value:

Not defined for shorthand properties (visible in CSS2.1)

Applies to:

Nonreplaced elements with a display value of block or inline-block

Inherited:

No

Computed value:

Same as declared value

Description:

A shorthand property that defines what happens to content that overflows the content area of an element. For the value scroll, user agents should provide a scrolling mechanism whether or not it is actually needed; for example, scrollbars would appear even if all content can fit within the element box. If two values are supplied, the first defines the value of overflow-x and the second defines overflow-y; otherwise a single value defines both.

Examples:

```
#masthead {overflow: hidden;}
object {overflow: visible scroll;}
```

Note:

In CSS2.1, overflow was a standalone property, not a shorthand property. As of mid-2011, no-display and no-content were not supported by any major browser.

---

overflow-x

Values:

visible | hidden | scroll | auto | no-display | no-content

Initial value:

visible

Applies to:

Nonreplaced elements with a display value of block or inline-block

Inherited:

No

Computed value:

Same as declared value

Description:

Defines the overflow behavior along the horizontal (X) axis of the element; that is, the left and right edges of the element.

Examples:

```
#masthead {overflow-x: hidden;}
object {overflow-x: visible;}
```

Note:

As of mid-2011, no-display and no-content were not supported by any major browser.

---

overflow-y

Values:

visible | hidden | scroll | auto | no-display | no-content

Initial value:

visible

Applies to:

Nonreplaced elements with a display value of block or inline-block

Inherited:

No

Computed value:

Same as declared value

Description:

Defines the overflow behavior along the vertical (Y) axis of the element; that is, the top and bottom edges of the element.

Examples:

```
#masthead {overflow-y: hidden;}
object {overflow-y: scroll;}
```

Note:

As of mid-2011, no-display and no-content were not supported by any major browser.

padding

Values:

[<length> | <percentage>]{1,4}

Initial value:

Not defined for shorthand elements

Applies to:

All elements

Inherited:

No

Percentages:

Refer to the width of the containing block

Computed value:

See individual properties

Description:

A shorthand property that defines the width of the overall padding for an element or sets the widths of each individual side's padding. Padding set on inline nonreplaced elements does not affect line-height calculations; therefore, such an element with both padding and a background may visibly extend into other lines and potentially overlap other content. The background of the element will extend throughout the padding. Negative padding values are not permitted.

Examples:

```
img {padding: 10px;}
h1 {padding: 2ex 0.33em;}
pre {padding: 0.75em 0.5em 1em 0.5em;}
```

padding-bottom

Values:

<length> | <percentage>

Initial value:

0

Applies to:

All elements

Inherited:

No

Percentages:

Refer to the width of the containing block

Computed value:

For percentage values, as declared; for length values, the absolute length

Description:

Defines the width of the bottom padding for an element. Bottom padding set on inline nonreplaced elements does not affect line-height calculations; therefore, such an element with both bottom padding and a background may visibly extend into other lines and potentially overlap other content. Negative padding values are not permitted.

Examples:

```
ul {padding-bottom: 0.5in;}
h1 {padding-bottom: 2%;}
```

padding-left

Values:

<length> | <percentage>

Initial value:

0

Applies to:

All elements

Inherited:

No

Percentages:

Refer to the width of the containing block

Computed value:

For percentage values, as declared; for length values, the absolute length

Description:

Defines the width of the left padding for an element. Left padding set for an inline nonreplaced element will appear only on the left edge of the first inline box generated by the element. Negative padding values are not permitted.

Examples:

```
p {padding-left: 5%;}
pre {padding-left: 3em;}
```

padding-right

Values:

<length> | <percentage>

Initial value:

0

Applies to:

All elements

Inherited:

No

Percentages:

Refer to the width of the containing block

Computed value:

For percentage values, as declared; for length values, the absolute length

Description:

Defines the width of the right padding for an element. Right padding set for an inline nonreplaced element will appear only on the right edge of the last inline box generated by the element. Negative padding values are not permitted.

Examples:

```
img {padding-right: 30px;}
ol {padding-right: 5em;}
```

padding-top

Values:

<length> | <percentage>

Initial value:

0

Applies to:

All elements

Inherited:

No

Percentages:

Refer to the width of the containing block

Computed value:

For percentage values, as declared; for length values, the absolute length

Description:

Defines the width of the top padding for an element. Top padding set on inline nonreplaced elements does not affect line-height calculations; therefore, such an element with both top padding and a background may visibly extend into other lines and potentially overlap other content. Negative padding values are not permitted.

Examples:

```
ul {padding-top: 0.5in;}
h3 {padding-top: 1.5em;}
```

perspective

Values:

none | <number>

Initial value:

Applies to:

Block-level and inline-level elements

Inherited:

No

Computed value:

Same as declared value

Description:

Defines the amount of apparent 3D perspective of an element's transformed children, but not for the element itself. Numbers define a foreshortening depth in pixels; smaller numbers define more extreme perspective effects. Negative values are treated the same as none.

Examples:

```
body {perspective: 250;} /* middlin' */
#wrapper {perspective: 10;} /* extreme */
```

Note:

As of early 2011, this property was only supported in a prefixed form by WebKit.

perspective-origin

Values:

[[<percentage> | <length> | left | center | right] [<percentage> | <length> | top | center | bottom]?] | [[left | center | right] || [top | center | bottom]]

Initial value:

50% 50%

Applies to:

Block-level and inline-level elements

Inherited:

No

Percentages:

Refer to the size of the element box

Computed value:

Same as declared value

Description:

Defines the origin point of the apparent 3D perspective within the element. In effect, it defines the point in the element that appears to be directly in front of the viewer.

Examples:

```
body {perspective-origin: bottom right;}
#wrapper div {perspective-origin: 0 50%;}
```

Note:

As of early 2011, this property was only supported in a prefixed form by WebKit.

position

Values:

static | relative | absolute | fixed

Initial value:

static

Applies to:

All elements

Inherited:

No

Computed value:

Same as declared value

Description:

Defines the positioning scheme used to lay out an element. Any element may be positioned, although an element positioned with absolute or fixed will generate a block-level box regardless of what kind of element it is. An element that is relatively positioned is offset from its default placement in the normal flow.

Examples:

```
#footer {position: fixed; bottom: 0;}
*.offset {position: relative; top: 0.5em;}
```

Note:

Fixed positioning is supported by Internet Explorer only in versions 7 and later.

quotes

Values:

[<string> <string>]+ | none

Initial value:

User agent–dependent

Applies to:

All elements (CSS2); all elements, ::before, ::after, ::alternate, ::marker, ::line-marker, margin areas, and @footnote areas (CSS3)

Inherited:

Yes

Computed value:

Same as declared value

Description:

Defines the quotation pattern used with quotes and nested quotes. The actual quote marks are inserted via the content property's open-quote and close-quote values. Note that several of the pseudo-elements to which quotes applies, such as ::alternate, ::marker, and ::line-marker, are new in CSS3 and may not be supported.

Example:

```
q {quotes: '\201C' '\201D' '\2018' '\2019';}
```

resize

Values:

none | both | horizontal | vertical

Initial value:

Applies to:

Elements whose `overflow` value is not `visible`

Inherited:

No

Computed value:

Same as declared value

Description:

Defines how (or whether) an element can be resized by the user. The actual appearance and operation of any resize mechanism is left to the user agent and is likely dependent on the writing direction.

Examples:

```
textarea {resize: vertical;}
iframe {resize: both;}
```

right

Values:

<length> | <percentage> | auto

Initial value:

auto

Applies to:

Positioned elements (that is, elements for which the value of `position` is something other than `static`)

Inherited:

No

Percentages:

Refer to the width of the containing block

Computed value:

For relatively positioned elements, see the note; for static elements, auto; for length values, the corresponding absolute length; for percentage values, the declared value; otherwise, auto.

Description:

Defines the offset between the right outer margin edge of a positioned element and the right edge of its containing block.

Examples:

```
div#footer {position: fixed; right: 0;}
*.overlapper {position: relative; right: -25px;}
```

Note:

For relatively positioned elements, the computed value of left always equals right.

---

ruby-align

Values:

auto | start | left | center | end | right | distribute-letter | distribute-space | line-edge

Initial value:

auto

Applies to:

All elements and generated content

Inherited:

Yes

Computed value:

Same as declared value

Description:

Defines the relative alignment of ruby text as compared to ruby base contents.

Examples:

```
ruby {ruby-align: start;}
rubytext {ruby-align: distribute-space;}
```

Note:

A "ruby" is a short run of text that goes alongside base text, which is common in written East Asian languages. As of early 2011, this property was supported only by Internet Explorer.

ruby-overhang

Values:

auto | start | end | none

Initial value:

Applies to:

The parent elements of elements with a display value of ruby-text

Inherited:

Yes

Computed value:

Same as declared value

Description:

Defines whether, and to which side of the base text, a ruby wider than its base text is allowed to overhang text adjacent to its base.

Examples:

```
rubytext {ruby-overhang: none;}
```

Note:

A "ruby" is a short run of text that goes alongside base text, which is common in written East Asian languages. As of early 2011, this property was supported only by Internet Explorer.

---

ruby-position

Values:

before | after | right

Initial value:

before

Applies to:

The parent elements of elements with a `display` value of `ruby-text`

Inherited:

Yes

Computed value:

Same as declared value

Description:

Defines the position of ruby text in relation to its base text.

Examples:

```
rubytext {ruby-position: before;}
```

Note:

A "ruby" is a short run of text that goes alongside base text, which is common in written East Asian languages. As of early 2011, this property was supported only by Internet Explorer.

---

ruby-span

Values:

attr(x) | none

Initial value:

Applies to:

Elements with a `display` value of `ruby-text`

Inherited:

No

Computed value:

A number

Description:

Defines the number of ruby base text elements that can be spanned by the ruby text. The attribute value must be a number and is evaluated as such. The values `0` and `none` are both equivalent to `1`, which indicates no spanning.

Examples:

```
rubytext {ruby-span: attr(span);}
```

Note:

A "ruby" is a short run of text that goes alongside base text, which is common in written East Asian languages. As of early 2011, this property was supported only by Internet Explorer.

table-layout

Values:

auto | fixed

Initial value:

auto

Applies to:

Elements with a `display` value of `table` or `inline-table`

Inherited:

No

Computed value:

Same as declared value

Description:

Defines whether a table element should be laid out using an automatic layout algorithm or a fixed-layout algorithm. The benefit of the automatic algorithm is that it's more like what authors are used to from more than a decade of browser behavior. The fixed-layout algorithm is theoretically faster and more predictable.

Examples:

```
table.data {table-display: fixed;}
table.directory {table-display: auto;}
```

text-align

CSS2 values:

left | center | right | justify | <string>

CSS2.1 values:

left | center | right | justify

CSS3 values:

[start | end | left | center | right | justify | match-parent] || <string>

Initial value:

User agent–specific, often based on writing direction (CSS2.1); start (CSS3)

Applies to:

Block-level elements

Inherited:

Yes

Computed value:

Same as declared value

Description:

Defines the horizontal alignment of text within a block-level element by defining the point to which line boxes are aligned. The value justify is supported by allowing user agents to programmatically adjust the word (but not letter) spacing of the line's content; results may vary by user agent.

Examples:

```
p {text-align: justify;}
h4 {text-align: center;}
```

Note:

CSS2 included a <string> value that was dropped from CSS2.1 because of a lack of support but returned in CSS3. As of mid-2011, it still lacked browser support.

---

text-decoration

Values:

none | [underline || overline || line-through || blink]

Initial value:

Applies to:

All elements

Inherited:

No

Computed value:

Same as declared value

Description:

Defines text-decoration effects such as underlining. These decorations will span descendant elements that don't have decorations of their own, in many cases making the child elements appear to be decorated. Combinations of the values are legal. Any time two text-decoration declarations apply to the same element, the values of the two declarations are *not* combined. For example:

```
h1 {text-decoration: overline;}
h1, h2 {text-decoration: underline;}
```

Given these styles, h1 elements will be underlined with no overline because the value of underline completely overrides the value of overline. If h1 should have both overlines and underlines, use the value overline underline for the h1 rule and move it after the h1, h2 rule or extend its selector to raise its specificity.

User agents are not required to support blink.

Examples:

```
u {text-decoration: underline;}
.old {text-decoration: line-through;}
u.old {text-decoration: line-through underline;}
```

---

text-indent

CSS2 Values:

<length> | <percentage>

CSS3 Values:

[<length> | <percentage>] && [hanging || each-line]?

Initial value:

0

Applies to:

Block-level elements

Inherited:

Yes

Percentages:

Refer to the width of the containing block

Computed value:

For percentage values, as declared; for length values, the absolute length

Description:

Defines the indentation of the first line of content in a block-level element. It is most often used to create a tab effect. Negative values are permitted and cause outdent (or hanging indent) effects. In CSS3, the value each-line will apply the indentation to any new line that results from a forced line break (e.g., due to a <br> element) within the element, not just the first line. The value hanging inverts the defined pattern of indentation, allowing for the creation of an outdent effect without using a negative length value.

Examples:

```
p {text-indent: 5em;}
h2 {text-indent: -25px;}
```

text-overflow

Values:

clip | ellipsis

Initial value:

clip

Applies to:

Block-level elements

Inherited:

No

Computed value:

Same as declared values

Description:

Defines the behavior when inline content overflows its parent element's box in cases where the parent element does not have an `overflow` value of `visible`. The default value is the historical behavior, where the content is simply clipped to the edges of the parent's box. The value `ellipsis` means the content should be clipped but an ellipsis (...) is inserted at or near the "end" of the element. In a top-to-bottom, left-to-right language such as English, this would place the ellipsis at or near the bottom-right corner of the element.

Examples:

```
pre {text-overflow: clip;}
article {text-overflow: ellipsis;}
```

text-shadow

Values:

none | [<length>{2,4} <color>?,] * <length>{2,4} <color>?

Initial value:

Applies to:

All elements

Inherited:

Yes

Computed value:

One or more sets of a color plus three absolute lengths

Description:

Defines one or more shadows to be "cast" by the text of an element. Shadows are always painted behind the element's text, but in front of the element's background, borders, and outline. Shadows are drawn from the first on top to the last on the bottom.

The four length values that can be declared are, in order: horizontal offset, vertical offset, blur distance, and spread distance. When positive, the offset values go down and to the right; when negative, back and to the left. Positive spread values increase the size of the shadow and negative values contract it. Blur values cannot be negative.

Examples:

```
h1 {text-shadow: 0.5em 0.33em 4px 2px gray;}
h2 {text-shadow: 0 -3px 0.5em blue;}
```

text-transform

Values:

uppercase | lowercase | capitalize | none

Initial value:

Applies to:

All elements

Inherited:

Yes

Computed value:

Same as declared value

Description:

Defines the pattern for changing the case of letters in an element, regardless of the case of the text in the document source. The determination of which letters are to be capitalized by the value capitalize is not precisely defined, as it depends on user agents knowing how to recognize a "word."

Examples:

```
h1 {text-transform: uppercase;}
.title {text-transform: capitalize;}
```

top

Values:

\<length\> | \<percentage\> | auto

Initial value:

auto

Applies to:

Positioned elements (that is, elements for which the value of `position` is something other than `static`)

Inherited:

No

Percentages:

Refer to the height of the containing block

Computed value:

For relatively positioned elements, see note; for `static` elements, `auto`; for length values, the corresponding absolute length; for percentage values, the declared value; otherwise, `auto`

Description:

Defines the offset between the top outer margin edge of a positioned element and the top edge of its containing block.

Note:

For relatively positioned elements, if both `top` and `bottom` are `auto`, their computed values are both 0; if one of them is `auto`, it becomes the negative of the other; if neither is `auto`, `bottom` becomes the negative of the value of `top`.

Examples:

```
#masthead {position: fixed; top: 0;}
sub {position: relative; top: 0.5em;
    vertical-align: baseline;}
```

transform

Values:

none | <transform-function> [<transform-function>]*

Expansions:

<transform-function>

See description.

Initial value:

Applies to:

Block- and inline-level elements

Inherited:

No

Computed value:

Same as declared value

Description:

Defines one or more transforms of an element. These transforms can occur in a 2D or a simulated 3D space, depending on how the transforms are declared.

The permitted values for <transform-function> are lengthy and complex. For a full list with minimalist descriptions, please consult *http://w3.org/TR/css3-3d-transforms/#transform-functions*.

Examples:

```
table th {transform: rotate(45deg);}
li {transform: scale3d(1.2,1.7,0.85);}
```

transform-origin

Values:

[[[<percentage> | <length> | left | center | right] [<percentage>
| <length> | top | center | bottom]?] <length>?] | [[[left | center |
right]] [top | center | bottom]] <length>?]

Initial value:

50% 50% 0

Applies to:

Block- and inline-level elements

Inherited:

No

Percentages:

Refer to the size of the element box

Computed value:

For <length>, an absolute length; otherwise a percentage

Description:

Defines the origin point for an element's transforms in either 2D or
simulated 3D space. The marked-as-optional <length> values are
what define a 3D origin point; without them, the value is necessarily
in 2D space.

Examples:

```
table th {transform-origin: bottom left;}
li {transform-origin: 10% 10px 10em;}
```

Note:

As of mid-2011, there were separate working drafts for 2D and 3D
transforms, each of which defined its own value syntax for
transform-origin. What is listed here is an attempt to harmonize
the two without having to write out two separate but nearly identical value syntaxes.

transform-style

Values:

flat | preserve-3d

Initial value:

flat

Applies to:

Block- and inline-level elements

Inherited:

No

Computed value:

Same as declared value

Description:

Defines whether an element transformed in simulated 3D space should have its children rendered using a flat style, thus putting them all in the same 2D plane as the element, or attempt to use a 3D effect where children with positive or negative z-index values may be rendered "in front of" or "behind" the element's plane as it rotates. Elements whose overflow value is hidden cannot preserve 3D effects and are treated as though the value of transform-style is flat.

Examples:

```
li {transform-style: preserve-3d;}
```

transition

Values:

[<'transition-property'> || <'transition-duration'> || <'transition-timing-function'> || <'transition-delay'> [, [<'transition-property'> || <'transition-duration'> || <'transition-timing-function'> || <'transition-delay'>]]*

Initial value:

Not defined for shorthand properties

Applies to:

All elements plus the ::before and ::after pseudo-elements

Inherited:

No

Computed value:

Same as declared value

Description:

A shorthand property that defines the aspects of one or more of an element's transitions from one state to another.

Even though it is not (as of this writing) explicitly defined in the value syntax, descriptive text in the specification defines that when two <time> values are declared, the first is the duration and the second is the delay. If only one is declared, it defines only the duration.

Examples:

```
a[href]:hover {transition: color 1s 0.25s ease-in-out;}
h1 {transition: linear all 10s;}
```

transition-delay

Values:

<time> [, <time>]*

Initial value:

0

Applies to:

All elements plus the ::before and ::after pseudo-elements

Inherited:

No

Computed value:

Same as declared value

Description:

Defines a delay between when a transition could theoretically first start and when it actually starts. For example, if a transition is defined to begin on hover but has a delay of 0.5s, the transition will actually begin half a second after the element is first hovered. Negative time values are permitted, but rather than creating a paradox, this simply jumps the transition to the point it would have reached had it been started at the defined time offset in the past. In other words, it will be started partway through the transition and run to its conclusion.

Examples:

```
a[href]:hover {transition-delay: 0.25;}
h1 {transition-delay: 0;}
```

---

transition-duration

Values:

<time> [, <time>]*

Initial value:

0

Applies to:

All elements plus the ::before and ::after pseudo-elements

Inherited:

No

Computed value:

Same as declared value

Description:

Defines the length of time it takes for the transition to run from start to finish. The default 0 means the transition is instantaneous and no animation occurs. Negative time values are treated as 0.

Examples:

```
a[href]:hover {transition-duration: 1s;}
h1 {transition-duration: 10s;}
```

transition-property

Values:

none | all | [<IDENT>] [',' <IDENT>]*

Initial value:

all

Applies to:

All elements plus the ::before and ::after pseudo-elements

Inherited:

No

Computed value:

Same as declared value

Description:

Defines one or more properties that are transitioned from one state to another; for example, color means that the foreground color of an element is transitioned from the start color to the finish color. If a shorthand property is declared, the transition parameters meant for that property are propagated to all the properties represented by the shorthand.

The keyword all means all properties are transitioned. The keyword none prevents any properties from being transitioned, effectively shutting down the transition.

Examples:

```
a[href]:hover {transition-property: color;}
h1 {transition-property: all;}
```

transition-timing-function

Values:

<transition-timing> [, <transition-timing>]*

Expansions:

<transition-timing>

ease | linear | ease-in | ease-out | ease-in-out | cubic-bezier(<number>, <number>, <number>, <number>)

Initial value:

ease

Applies to:

All elements plus the ::before and ::after pseudo-elements

Inherited:

No

Computed value:

Same as declared value

Description:

Defines the way in which intermediate states of a transition are calculated. The value keywords (ease, linear, etc.) are shorthands for specific cubic-bezier() values defined in the specification, so in effect all values of this property are cubic-bezier() values.

Examples:

```
a[href]:hover {transition-timing-function: ease-in-out;}
h1 {transition-timing-function: linear;}
```

unicode-bidi

Values:

normal | embed | bidi-override

Initial value:

normal

Applies to:

All elements

Inherited:

No

Computed value:

Same as declared value

Description:

Allows the author to generate levels of embedding within the unicode bidirectional algorithm. User agents that do not support bidirectional text are permitted to ignore this property.

Examples:

```
span.name {direction: rtl; unicode-bidi: embed;}
```

vertical-align

Values:

baseline | sub | super | top | text-top | middle | bottom | text-bottom | <percentage> | <length>

Initial value:

baseline

Applies to:

Inline elements and table cells

Inherited:

No

Percentages:

Refer to the value of line-height for the element

Computed value:

For percentage and length values, the absolute length; otherwise, same as declared value

Description:

Defines the vertical alignment of an inline element's baseline with respect to the baseline of the line in which it resides. Negative length and percentage values are permitted, and they lower the element instead of raising it.

In table cells, this property sets the alignment of the content of the cell within the cell box. When applied to table cells, only the values baseline, top, middle, and bottom are recognized.

Examples:

```
sup {vertical-align: super;}
.fnote {vertical-align: 50%;}
```

visibility

Values:

visible | hidden | collapse

Initial value:

inherit

Applies to:

All elements

Inherited:

No

Computed value:

Same as declared value

Description:

Defines whether the element box generated by an element is rendered. This means authors can have the element take up the space it would ordinarily take up, while remaining completely invisible. The value `collapse` is used in tables to remove columns or rows from the table's layout.

Examples:

```
ul.submenu {visibility: hidden;}
tr.hide {visibility: collapse;}
```

white-space

Values:

normal | nowrap | pre | pre-wrap | pre-line

Initial value:

normal

Applies to:

All elements (CSS2.1); block-level elements (CSS2)

Inherited:

No

Computed value:

Same as declared value

Description:

Defines how whitespace within an element is handled during layout. `normal` acts as web browsers have traditionally treated text, in that it reduces any sequence of whitespace to a single space. `pre` causes whitespace to be treated as in the HTML element `pre`, with both whitespace and line breaks fully preserved. `nowrap` prevents an element from line-breaking, as in the "nowrap" attribute for `td` and th elements in HTML4. The values `pre-wrap` and `pre-line` were added in CSS2.1; the former causes the user agent to preserve whitespace while still automatically wrapping lines of text, and the latter honors newline characters within the text while collapsing all other whitespace as per `normal`.

Examples:
```
td {white-space: nowrap;}
tt {white-space: pre;}
```

width

Values:

<length> | <percentage> | auto

Initial value:

auto

Applies to:

Block-level and replaced elements

Inherited:

No

Percentages:

Refer to the width of the containing block

Computed value:

For auto and percentage values, as declared; otherwise, an absolute length, unless the property does not apply to the element (then auto)

Description:

Defines the width of an element's content area, outside of which padding, borders, and margins are added. This property is ignored for inline nonreplaced elements. Negative length and percentage values are not permitted.

Examples:

```
table {width: 80%;}
#sidebar {width: 20%;}
.figure img {width: 200px;}
```

word-spacing

Values:

[normal | <length> | <percentage>]{1,3}

Initial value:

normal

Applies to:

All elements

Inherited:

Yes

Percentages:

Refer to the width of the Unicode space glyph (U+0020) of the element's font face

Computed value:

For length values, the absolute length; otherwise, normal

Description:

Defines the amount of whitespace to be inserted between words. Note that the specification does not define what constitutes a "word." In typical practice, user agents will apply this to the collapsed whitespace between strings of nonwhitespace characters. Negative length values are permitted and will cause words to bunch closer together.

Examples:

```
p.spacious {letter-spacing: 6px;}
em {letter-spacing: 0.2em;}
p.cramped {letter-spacing: -0.5em;}
```

Note:

In CSS2.1, word-spacing only accepts a single value: either a
<length> or normal.

word-wrap

Values:

normal | break-word

Initial value:

normal

Applies to:

All elements

Inherited:

Yes

Computed value:

Same as declared value

Description:

Defines how text should be wrapped in situations where it would
not ordinarily be wrapped; for example, a very long string of numbers containing no spaces, such as the first thousand digits of pi.
The value break-word permits user agents to break a word at arbitrary points if it cannot find regular breakpoints within the "word"
(text string).

Examples:

```
td {word-wrap: break-word;}
p {word-wrap: normal;}
```

z-index

Values:

<integer> | auto

Initial value:

auto

Applies to:

Positioned elements

Inherited:

No

Computed value:

Same as declared value

Description:

Defines the placement of a positioned element along the z-axis, which is defined to be the axis that extends perpendicular to the display area. Positive numbers are closer to the user, and negative numbers are farther away.

Example:

```
#masthead {position: relative; z-index: 10000;}
```

Paged Media

break-after

Values:

auto | always | avoid | left | right | page | column | avoid-page | avoid-column

Initial value:

auto

Applies to:

Block-level elements

Inherited:

No

Computed value:

Same as declared value

Description:

Defines whether a column or page break should or should not be placed after the element. Although it is theoretically possible to force breaks with `always`, it is not possible to guarantee prevention; the best an author can do is ask the user agent to `avoid` inserting a column or page break after the element. The keywords `avoid-column` and `avoid-page` attempt to prevent insertion after the element of column or page breaks, respectively. The keyword `left` is used to insert enough breaks after the element to make the next page be a left-hand page; similarly, `right` is used for a right-hand page. `page` and `always` insert a page break after the element; `column` and `always`, a column break.

Examples:

```
h3 {break-after: avoid;}
div.col {break-after: column;}
```

break-before

Values:

auto | always | avoid | left | right | page | column | avoid-page | avoid-column

Initial value:

auto

Applies to:

Block-level elements

Inherited:

No

Computed value:

Same as declared value

Description:

Defines whether a column or page break should or should not be placed before the element. Although it is theoretically possible to force breaks with `always`, it is not possible to guarantee prevention; the best an author can do is ask the user agent to `avoid` inserting a column or page break before the element. The keywords `avoid-column` and `avoid-page` attempt to prevent insertion before the element of column or page breaks, respectively. The keyword `left` is used to insert enough breaks before the element to make the page be a left-hand page; similarly, `right` is used for a right-hand page. `page` and `always` insert a page break before the element; `column` and `always`, a column break.

Examples:

```
h2 {break-before: always;}
h3 {break-before: avoid;}
```

break-inside

Values:

auto | avoid | avoid-page | avoid-column

Initial value:

auto

Applies to:

Block-level elements

Inherited:

No

Computed value:

Same as declared value

Description:

Defines whether a column or page break should be avoided within the element. Note that such avoidance may not be possible; for example, declaring body {break-inside: avoid-page;} for a lengthy document will not prevent the insertion of page breaks by the user agent.

Examples:

```
table {break-inside: avoid;}
ul {break-inside: avoid-column;}
```

---

image-orientation

Values:

auto | <angle>

Initial value:

auto

Applies to:

Image elements

Inherited:

N/A

Computed value:

Same as declared value

Description:

Defines a clockwise rotation angle for images when displayed in paged media. The intent is to allow authors to rotate images that may have come from devices such as cell phones that do not automatically rotate images that are taken "sideways." User agents are required to support angle values that compute to 0deg, 90deg, 180deg, and 270deg. Other angle values may be ignored. Note that the property is *not* needed to rotate images when switching from portrait to landscape layout or vice versa; such rotation should be done automatically by the user agent.

Examples:

```
img.oldphone {image-orientation: 90deg;}
```

marks

Values:

[crop || cross] | none

Initial value:

Applies to:

The page context

Inherited:

No

Computed value:

Same as declared value

Description:

Defines whether cross or crop marks should be added to the display of a page.

Examples:

```
@page {marks: cross crop;}
```

orphans

Values:

<integer>

Initial value:

2

Applies to:

Block-level elements

Inherited:

Yes

Computed value:

Same as declared value

Description:

Defines the minimum number of text lines within an element that can be left at the bottom of a page. This can affect the placement of page breaks within the element.

Examples:

```
p {orphans: 4;}
ul {orphans: 2;}
```

page

Values:

auto | <identifier>

Initial value:

auto

Applies to:

Block-level elements

Inherited:

Yes

Computed value:

Same as declared value

Description:

Defines the page type that *should* be used when displaying the element. The emphasis of the word "should" is taken directly from the specification, so author beware.

The intended effect is that if an element has a value of page that is different than that of the preceding element, at least one page break is inserted before the element and a new page started using the page type declared by page. (Multiple page breaks may be used if other styles call for using a right- or left-hand page when starting the new page.)

Examples:

```
@page wide {size: landscape;}
table.summary {page: wide;}
```

page-break-after

Values:

auto | always | avoid | left | right

Initial value:

auto

Applies to:

Block-level elements

Inherited:

No

Computed value:

Same as declared value

Description:

Defines whether one or more page breaks should be placed after an element. Although it is theoretically possible to force breaks with always, it is not possible to guarantee prevention; avoid asks the user agent to avoid inserting a page break if possible. The keyword left is used to insert enough breaks after the element to make the next page be a left-hand page; similarly, right is used for a right-hand page.

This property is essentially replaced by break-after, but browser support for page-break-after may be stronger.

Examples:

```
section {page-break-after: always;}
h1 {page-break-after: avoid;}
```

page-break-before

Values:

auto | always | avoid | left | right

Initial value:

auto

Applies to:

Block-level elements

Inherited:

No

Computed value:

Same as declared value

Description:

Defines whether one or more page breaks should be placed before an element. Although it is theoretically possible to force breaks with always, it is not possible to guarantee prevention; avoid asks the user agent to avoid inserting a page break if possible. The keyword left is used to insert enough breaks before the element to make the page be a left-hand page; similarly, right is used for a right-hand page.

This property is essentially replaced by break-before, but browser support for page-break-before may be stronger.

Examples:

```
section {page-break-before: always;}
h2 {page-break-before: avoid;}
```

page-break-inside

Values:

auto | avoid

Initial value:

auto

Applies to:

Block-level elements

Inherited:

No

Computed value:

Same as declared value

Description:

Defines whether a page break should be avoided within the element. Note that such avoidance may not be possible; for example, declaring body {page-break-inside: avoid;} for a lengthy document will not prevent the insertion of page breaks by the user agent.

This property is essentially replaced by break-inside, but browser support for page-break-inside may be stronger.

Examples:

    table {page-break-inside: avoid;}

page-policy

Values:

start | first | last

Initial value:

start

Applies to:

@counter and @string blocks

Inherited:

N/A

Computed value:

Same as declared value

Description:

Defines how to determine the value of a counter or string value with regards to a page-based element. For example, an author may define a CSS counter to express section numbers. The author then might want to have the header of every page contain the section number of the first section found on each page. This would be done using @counter secnum {page-policy: first;} (plus related CSS needed to create the counter pattern). If the desire is to use the last instance of the counter on the page, then page-policy: last would be used instead. The value start uses the value before anything is done with the page; to continue the example, it would use the counter number as carried over from the previous page, not the first instance of the counter on the current page.

Examples:

```
@counter chapter {page-policy: first;}
@string section-title {page-policy: start;}
```

---

size

Values:

auto | <length>{1,2} | [<page-size> || [portrait | landscape]]

Expansions:

<page-size>

A5 | A4 | A3 | B5 | B4 | letter | legal | ledger

Initial value:

auto

Applies to:

The page context

Inherited:

N/A

Computed value:

Same as declared value

Description:

Defines the size and orientation of a page box. The keywords `auto`, `portrait`, and `landscape` cause the page box to fill the available rendering space on the page. Page boxes set to `portrait` have the content printed with the long sides of the page box being the right and left sides; in the case of `landscape`, the content is printed with the longer sides of the page box being the top and bottom sides.

If a page box is specified using lengths or one of the <page-size> keywords (e.g., A4) and the page box cannot be fit onto the actual page used for display, the page box and its contents may be scaled down to fit. If only one length value is declared, it sets both dimensions and thus defines a square page box. Length values that use `em` or `ex` units are calculated with respect to the computed font size of the page context.

Examples:

```
body {page-size: landscape;}
```

widows

Values:

<integer>

Initial value:

2

Applies to:

Block-level elements

Inherited:

Yes

Computed value:

Same as declared value

Description:

Defines the minimum number of text lines within an element that can be left at the top of a page. This can affect the placement of page breaks within the element.

Examples:

```
p {widows: 4;}
ul {widows: 2;}
```

Aural Media

---

cue

Values:

<'cue-before'> || <'cue-after'>

Initial value:

Not defined for shorthand properties

Applies to:

All elements

Inherited:

No

Percentages:

Apply to the inherited value for voice-volume

Computed value:

See individual properties (cue-before, etc.)

Description:

A shorthand property that defines audio cues that precede and follow the audio rendering of an element's content. A cue is something like an auditory icon.

Examples:

```
table.layout {
    cue: url(shattered-glass.ogg) url(sad-trombone.wav);}
pre {cue: url(raygun.mp3);}
```

---

cue-after

Values:

none | <uri> [<number> | <percentage> | silent | x-soft | soft | medium | loud | x-loud]

Initial value:

Applies to:

All elements

Inherited:

No

Percentages:

Apply to the inherited value for voice-volume

Computed value:

For <uri> values, the absolute URI; otherwise, none

Description:

Defines an audio cue that follows the audio rendering of an element's content.

Examples:

```
table.layout {cue-after: url(sad-trombone.wav);}
pre {cue-after: url(raygun.mp3);}
```

---

cue-before

Values:

none | \<uri> [\<number> | \<percentage> | silent | x-soft | soft | medium | loud | x-loud]

Initial value:

Applies to:

All elements

Inherited:

No

Percentages:

Apply to the inherited value for voice-volume

Computed value:

For \<uri> values, the absolute URI; otherwise, none

Description:

Defines an audio cue that precedes the audio rendering of an element's content.

Examples:

```
table.layout {cue-before: url(shattered-glass.ogg);}
pre {cue-before: url(raygun.mp3);}
```

pause

Values:

\<'pause-before'> || \<'pause-after'>

Initial value:

Not defined for shorthand properties

Applies to:

All elements

Inherited:

No

Computed value:

See individual properties

Description:

A shorthand property that defines pauses that precede and follow the audio rendering of an element's content. A pause is an interval in which no content is audibly rendered, although background sounds may still be audible. See pause-before and pause-after for details on the placement of the pauses.

Examples:

```
h1 {pause: 1s 500ms;}
ul {pause: 250ms;}
```

pause-after

Values:

none | x-weak | weak | medium | strong | x-strong | <time>

Initial value:

User agent–dependent

Applies to:

All elements

Inherited:

No

Computed value:

The absolute time value

Description:

Defines the length of a pause that follows the audio rendering of an element's content. A pause is an interval in which no content is audibly rendered, although background sounds may still be audible. The pause is rendered after any cue that follows the element (see cue-after and related properties).

Examples:

```
h1 {pause-after: 500ms;}
ul {pause-after: 250ms;}
```

pause-before

Values:

none | x-weak | weak | medium | strong | x-strong | <time>

Initial value:

User agent–dependent

Applies to:

All elements

Inherited:

No

Computed value:

The absolute time value

Description:

Defines the length of a pause that precedes the audio rendering of an element's content. A pause is an interval in which no content is audibly rendered, although background sounds may still be audible. The pause is rendered before any cue that precedes the element (see cue-before and related properties).

Examples:

```
h1 {pause-before: 1s;}
ul {pause-before: 250ms;}
```

phonemes

Values:

<string>

Initial value:

User agent–dependent

Applies to:

All elements

Inherited:

No

Computed value:

Not specified, but likely as declared

Description:

Defines a phonetic pronunciation for the content of the element. The <string> value uses the International Phonetic Alphabet by way of escaped Unicode codepoints.

Examples:

```
#tomato {phonemes: "t\0252 m\0251 to\028a ";}
```

rest

Values:

<'rest-before'> || <'rest-after'>

Initial value:

Not defined for shorthand properties

Applies to:

All elements

Inherited:

No

Computed value:

Not specified, but likely a pair of absolute time values

Description:

A shorthand property that defines rests that precede and follow the audio rendering of an element's content. A rest is an interval in which no content is audibly rendered, although background sounds may still be audible. See `rest-before` and `rest-after` for details on the placement of the rests.

Examples:

```
th {rest: 0.5s;}
strong {rest: 333ms 250ms;}
```

rest-after

Values:

none | x-weak | weak | medium | strong | x-strong | <time>

Initial value:

User agent–dependent

Applies to:

All elements

Inherited:

No

Computed value:

Not specified, but likely an absolute time value

Description:

Defines the length of a rest that follows the audio rendering of an element's content. A rest is an interval in which no content is audibly rendered, although background sounds may still be audible.

The rest is rendered after the element's content but before any cue that follows the element (see cue-after and related properties).

Examples:

```
th {rest-after: 0.5s;}
strong {rest-after: 250ms;}
```

rest-before

Values:

none | x-weak | weak | medium | strong | x-strong | <time>

Initial value:

User agent–dependent

Applies to:

All elements

Inherited:

No

Computed value:

Not specified, but likely an absolute time value

Description:

Defines the length of a rest that precedes the audio rendering of an element's content. A rest is an interval in which no content is audibly rendered, although background sounds may still be audible. The rest is rendered before the element's content but after any cue that precedes the element (see cue-before and related properties).

Examples:

```
th {rest-before: 0.5s;}
strong {rest-before: 333ms;}
```

speak

Values:

normal | spell-out | digits | literal-punctuation | no-punctuation

Initial value:

normal

Applies to:

All elements

Inherited:

Yes

Computed value:

Not specified

Description:

Defines how an element's contents will be audibly rendered. The value spell-out is typically used for acronyms and abbreviations, such as W3C or CSS. Declaring digits means that numbers are spoken one digit at a time; for example, the number 13 is spoken as "one three." The value literal-punctuation causes punctuation marks to be spoken literally, as in the words "period" and "semicolon"; no-punctuation causes punctuation to be skipped entirely and no pauses are rendered in their place.

Examples:

```
abbr {speak: spell-out;}
*.tel {speak: digits;}
```

speakability

Values:

auto | none | normal

Initial value:

Applies to:

All elements

Inherited:

Yes

Computed value:

Not specified

Description:

Defines whether an element's contents will be rendered aurally. If the value is normal, the element is aurally rendered regardless of the value of display. If the value is none, the element, including any cues, pauses, or rests associated with the element, is skipped (takes no time to be audibly rendered). However, descendant elements may override the value, causing them to be aurally rendered. The value auto resolves to none if the value of display is none; otherwise it resolves to normal.

Examples:

```
abbr {speak: spell-out;}
*.tel {speak: digits;}
```

voice-balance

Values:

<number> | left | center | right | leftwards | rightwards

Initial value:

center

Applies to:

All elements

Inherited:

Yes

Computed value:

Not specified, but most likely an absolute number

Description:

Defines the stereo balancing of a speaking voice. This allows a voice to be shifted all the way to one side or the other, or (with a <number>) some mix of the two sides. For example, -50 would cause the voice to sound as if it is coming from the center-left position. <number> values are constrained to the range –100 to 100, inclusive. The keyword left is equivalent to -100; right to 100. The keyword leftwards subtracts 20 from the inherited value of voice-balance; rightwards add 20.

This property applies to audio cues (see cue and related properties).

Examples:

```
.beck {voice-balance: right;}
.moore {voice-balance: left;}
```

voice-duration

Values:

<time>

Initial value:

User agent–dependent

Applies to:

All elements

Inherited:

No

Computed value:

Not specified

Description:

Defines the length of time it should take to audibly render the content of the element. The result will override the value of voice-rate. Only positive <time> values are permitted.

Examples:

```
.tel {voice-duration: 3s;}
big {voice-duration: 10s;}
```

voice-family

Values:

<voice> [, <voice>]*

Expansions:

<voice>

<specific-voice> | [<age>? <generic-voice> <non-negative-number>?]

<age>

child | young | old

<generic-voice>

male | female | neutral

Initial value:

User agent–dependent

Applies to:

All elements

Inherited:

Yes

Computed value:

Same as declared value

Description:

Defines one or more voice families that can be used in the audio rendering of an element's content. It is comparable to font-family in that it can be used to supply a list of families, including generic alternatives.

Examples:

```
body {voice-family:
    "Karla", "Jenny", young female, female, neutral;}
small {voice-family: male child, child;}
```

voice-pitch

Values:

<number> | <percentage> | x-low | low | medium | high | x-high

Initial value:

medium

Applies to:

All elements

Inherited:

Yes

Percentages:

Refer to the inherited value

Computed value:

Not specified, but likely an absolute number

Description:

Defines the average pitch (frequency) of the speaking voice used to audibly render the element's content. The average pitch of a voice will depend greatly on the voice family. <number> values define an average pitch in hertz.

Examples:

```
big {voice-pitch: 100;}
small {voice-pitch: high;}
```

voice-pitch-range

Values:

<number> | <percentage> | x-low | low | medium | high | x-high

Initial value:

User agent–dependent

Applies to:

All elements

Inherited:

Yes

Percentages:

Refer to the inherited value

Computed value:

Not specified, but likely an absolute number

Description:

Defines the variation in average pitch used by the speaking voice while audibly rendering the element's content. The higher the variation, the more animated the voice will sound. <number> values define a pitch range in hertz.

Examples:

```
em {voice-pitch-range: high;}
code {voice-pitch-range: 50;}
```

voice-rate

Values:

<percentage> | x-slow | slow | medium | fast | x-fast

Initial value:

medium

Applies to:

All elements

Inherited:

Yes

Percentages:

Refer to the default value

Computed value:

Not specified (in the previous incarnation, speech-rate, it was an absolute number)

Description:

Defines the average rate at which words are spoken when an element's content is audibly rendered.

Examples:

```
h1 {voice-rate: 33%;}
.legalese {voice-rate: x-fast;}
```

voice-stress

Values:

strong | moderate | reduced | none

Initial value:

moderate

Applies to:

All elements

Inherited:

Yes

Computed value:

Not specified (but likely the declared value)

Description:

Affects the height of peaks in the intonation of a speaking voice, which are in turn generated by stress marks within a language.

Examples:

```
strong {voice-stress: strong;}
footer {voice-stress: reduced;}
```

voice-volume

Values:

<number> | <percentage> | silent | x-soft | soft | medium | loud | x-loud

Initial value:

medium

Applies to:

All elements

Inherited:

Yes

Percentages:

Refer to the inherited value

Computed value:

Not specified (in the previous incarnation, volume, it was an absolute number)

Description:

Defines the median volume level for the waveform of the audibly rendered content. Thus, a waveform with large peaks and valleys may go well above or below the volume level set with this property. <number> values are clipped to the range of 0 to 100, inclusive. Note that 0 is the same as silent and 100 is the same as x-loud.

Examples:

```
big {voice-volume: x-loud;}
footer {voice-volume: 15;}
```

Index

We'd like to hear your suggestions for improving our indexes. Send email to *index@oreilly.com*.